LOST IN IDEOLOGY

LOST IN IDEOLOGY

Interpreting Modern Political Life

Jason Blakely

agenda
publishing

First published in 2024 by Agenda Publishing
Reprinted 2024 (twice), 2025 (twice)

Agenda Publishing Limited
PO Box 185
Newcastle upon Tyne
NE20 2DH

www.agendapub.com

ISBN 978-1-78821-662-3 (hardcover)
ISBN 978-1-78821-663-0 (paperback)

British Library Cataloguing-in-Publication Data
A catalogue record for this book is available
from the British Library

Typeset in Nocturne by Patty Rennie

Printed and bound in the UK by 4edge Ltd

EU GPSR authorised representative:
Logos Europe, 9 rue Nicolas Poussin, 17000 La Rochelle, France
contact@logoseurope.eu

For Charles Taylor: the better maker.

Contents

Contents

"... Later generations, less addicted to the study of cartography, realized this enormous map was useless and not without some impiety handed it over to the severities of the sun and the winters".

Jorge Luis Borges, "On Rigor in Science", *The Maker* (1960)

Introduction: in search of ideology

What is ideology? The answer is simple, if you do not think about it very hard. Ideology is politics in excess – distorted, immoderate and delusional. It is pundits shouting at each other and unruly mobs chanting in the streets. It is an uncle ranting about socialism at holiday dinners or a co-worker lowering his voice to whisper about the dangers of "the system". Facts are of no avail when dealing with the victims of ideology; rational arguments slide off their brains like rain running down a granite dome.

As part of this, it has also become an unspoken rule to avoid describing your own politics as ideological. Respectable political ideas are best labelled a "belief system", "theory", "philosophy", or even plain old "common sense".[1] This is because your own politics are obviously reasonable and good, while those of an adversary are demonstrably irrational and false. If you are progressive, "ideology" is what coerces millions of people into conformity with inherited hierarchies and strips individuals of their freedom and well-being. If you are a conservative, "ideology" is a systematic attempt to replace the traditional moral order with faddish and radical ideas that eventually lead to societal decline and collapse. For both sides, escaping ideology is as simple as switching teams and adopting the one-and-only true and defensible politics.

The result of all this confusion and mutual accusation – as the American anthropologist Clifford Geertz brilliantly summed up – is "the term 'ideology' has itself become thoroughly ideologized".[2] Ideology is a snake swallowing its own tail; it is an idea that consumes itself. Indeed, what many people think of as the obvious definition of ideology is nothing more than one more flower growing inside their ideological garden. Every time we seek to rein in ideology, we end up expanding its scope.

But why are we all so confident that our own convictions are immune to the very ideology plainly afflicting everyone else? This book begins from the deceptively straightforward claim that part of our problem is we have forgotten that politics is cultural. Instead, we have conferred natural or even quasi-scientific status on our own preferred vision of society. We are *lost in ideology* because our particular map (cartography) is mistaken for brutely given nature (geography). We are like those mapmakers in Jorge Luis Borges's story, trying to draft a map of the empire that is the same size as the empire.[3] Ideologies are akin to a map that carpets over the surrounding land point by point. When this happens, we no longer appreciate the difference between our hopes and visions for society and the inescapable realities of the world.

I will also try to show that ideologies are not merely distortive in this way but at the same time illuminating for interpreting and navigating social reality. As with maps, there is this dual, contradictory potential to ideology. Namely, ideology in the modern era both orients and disorients – one must learn to read its markings and symbols properly. This book is an attempt to teach readers how to get their bearings amid the major ideological maps and within the mapmaking project of ideology more generally. As we shall see, without ideology we would not be able to decode our own cultures or even ourselves.

THE TENDENCY TO LOSE OUR WAY

Historians believe that in 1626 Peter Minuit, Director of New Netherland, purchased the island of Manhattan from some members of the Lenape tribe for 60 guilders worth of trade goods like kettles, hoes and axes. The island that eventually became the hub for global capital was initially acquired not by military conquest, but by the seventeenth-century equivalent of a real estate deal. Such wheeling and dealing would have made perfect sense within the ideological world of Dutch market society, with its adage that "Christ is good, but trade is better".[4] But was it intelligible within the cultural coordinates of the Lenape tribe?

After all, historians have argued that the Lenape recognized a communal "right to hunt, fish, and plant within certain territorial limits" but did not practice the "sale or permanent alienation" of land "known to European law".[5] Instead, the Lenape likely saw themselves as accepting gifts from the Dutch, entitling the latter to some shared use of Manhattan. They almost certainly would not have thought they were making final transfer of the dwelling place of their ancestors.

Of course, some members of the Dutch trading company may have detected that the entire transaction was bogus and cynically proceeded with the sale all the same. But others likely suffered from an ideological blind spot that persists today: namely, that the transaction was the result of common sense and that they were simply smarter than the dupes on the other side of the negotiation table. The deal would have appeared to such individuals as sharp business acumen. If Rome had its Romulus, the North American colonies had countless Peter Minuits, transferring the enchanted tribal lands of the mythic ancestors into the commodity parcels of the business-savvy colonists. The era of ideologies had arrived to the New World.

In this way, the "Age of Discovery" was already one of profound ideological confusion. Like Borges's mapmakers, the Dutch traders had unfurled their cartographic grid over all the territories and peoples of the New World, cutting off contact with the underlying indigenous culture. This experience of being disconnected from an alien culture is now nearly universal in our society, as we struggle to understand not a foreign tribe but our own neighbours, fellow citizens, colleagues and family members. Similar to the Dutch colonists, our own ideology seems to always arrive one step before us, as if it were an invisible carpet unrolling at our feet. As I will show in these pages, every ideological tradition is capable of generating this weird bewilderment – from conservatism to progressivism, nationalism to feminism. Ideology's labyrinth exists inside every politics.

IDEOLOGIES AS STORIES AND MAPS

We are meaning-making animals and ideologies are stories about the significance or meaning of social and political life.[6] This might sound like an uncontroversial claim. After all, who could reasonably deny that humans are meaning-makers seeking out the stories that most resonate with their own experiences? But one underappreciated consequence of this insight is that ideologies are cultural. They emerge from inside human language and history, and are not simply discovered within nature the way one spots the rings around Saturn or observes the migratory patterns of birds.

If ideologies are a form of meaning-making, then they are not so different from other forms of cultural production – theatre, literature, sports, cuisine, and music – that need to be understood through careful interpretation. Everyone knows that comprehending a rich story (say, one told by Homer or Shakespeare) requires a careful and patient art of interpretation. Yet comparatively few people are willing to lavish this kind of interpretive attention and generosity on ideology. This is especially true in cases where we find the other person's ideology confusing, off-putting, or even morally repugnant. Instead, the common tendency is to dismiss a rival's ideology as the product of some more basic mechanism like demographic identity, class interests, or even a psychological hang up.

Yet, if ideologies are stories, they cannot be fairly treated in this way but must be listened to on their own terms. As with a story, one gets the hang of an ideology and can grow more or less familiar with it by immersing oneself in interpreting its particular world, characters, language and plot. The more conversant one becomes in an ideology, the less likely one is to race to simplistic and reductive explanations. Likewise, the more conversant one becomes in multiple ideologies, the less prone one is to treat a favoured politics as natural or obvious.

In these pages I hope to help readers gain some fluency in a range of ideologies that are not their own. Each chapter is an attempt to achieve what Geertz called a "thick description" of an ideological tradition.[7] Geertz was a master of the method of ethnography, in which researchers immerse themselves for months and even years in foreign cultures. He spent countless hours embedded in distant tribal cultures – in Bali, Sumatra and Morocco – patiently observing, listening and learning. "Thick description" was his name for an account of a culture nuanced enough to be recognized by its own adherents as faithful to it.

Today, thick description needs to be brought back home in order to understand our closest neighbours, who may be geographically near but have grown culturally very distant. For this reason, in these pages each major ideology is presented through its most articulate champions. This often means looking at texts in which an ideology was originally given voice by a formidable philosopher or theorist. These leading figures bring into language what ordinary rank-and-file members recognize as the most nuanced and enduring versions of their own politics.

Ideologies are stories but they can also be thought of as what Geertz called "maps of problematic social reality".[8] Such maps help orient people within political space – not merely existing as narratives on a page but guiding their actions and practices, helping them to move in the world. Ideologies, for better or worse, are powerful sense-making aids. Often when someone adopts an ideology, they have a deep experience of something going "click" and might even feel a kind of exhilaration, as they think: "Aha! Now I finally understand politics! I know what steps to take and in which direction!"[9]

As stories and maps, ideologies must be allowed to speak to some extent in their own voice. This can be difficult not only due to the effort and disorientation which thinking through a rival ideology requires, but also because all ideologies contain within them a call or effort at recruitment. Not listening to a rival is sometimes the easiest way to deal with this temptation from the other side. Avoiding a rival's maps and stories also serves the political goal of establishing one's own ideology as hegemonic. But as students of ideology, we must avoid such false certainties. We must be willing to keep our ears open to strange voices and tales, even if like Odysseus this means tying ourselves to the mast as the sirens sing their perilous songs.

IDEOLOGIES AS LIQUID AND WORLDMAKING

Ideologies are maps, but this metaphor has limits. After all, conventional maps are frozen snapshots of the world. There is a risk that if we picture ideologies as maps, we will assume they are similarly static. However, the truth is ideologies are liquid and always changing. The liquidity of ideologies means it is a mistake to attribute to them ahistorical, core features. Instead, as the great scholar of ideologies Michael Freeden observed, ideologies consist of "family resemblances", with no single element remaining constant across all members.[10] As we shall see, the result is there is not one liberalism but many liberalisms, not one conservatism but many conservatisms, not one socialism but many socialisms, and so on.

Liquids do not have hard edges or solid borders and neither do ideologies. They can mix and blend in unexpected ways. Indeed, many strange hybrids appear in these pages – fascists who go green; socialists who favour gradualism; conservatives who reject capitalism; and much more. Many people know culture can hybridize (fusion cuisines, hybrid sports, syncretized religions, cross-genre musicians, etc.), but when it comes to ideology, all awareness of this permeability vanishes. Rather, the dominant view of ideologies is as a uniform left–right spectrum in which only neighbouring ideologies resemble or overlap with one another. Yet this is false. Any ideology can mix with any other. But to see this, readers must learn to *liquify* ideology.

Instead of a rigid scale – with discreet intervals like beads running along a string – liquid ideologies are similar to the action paintings of Jackson Pollock. In Pollock's complex splatter paintings, colours recur as drips, streaks and threads crisscrossing, weaving and bluring with other colours. A pattern of left to right may or may not emerge beneath the tumult, but the idea that left and right cannot combine in unexpected ways is a myth that contributes to the current disorientation.

In addition to rejecting the picture of ideologies as static, the metaphor of maps also needs to be updated to avoid thinking of ideologies as simply descriptive of a world "out there". Conventional maps deploy symbols to represent a reality that is separate from what is on the page. If a cartographer edits a map of Yosemite, moving a peak or recharting a ridge, there is no way in which the mountains themselves stand up and move. By contrast, ideological maps always have the potential to reposition the very political landscape they sometimes appear to be describing. In other words, ideologies are *worldmaking* and a creative enough cartographer can move mountains if the multitudes join in putting their backs into the work.

Ideological maps, therefore, conjure forth and help build social reality.[11] This is because ideological meanings and symbols can be embodied in practices, institutions, laws, economies, regimes, and forms of self. A common way to become lost in ideology is when everything in a social world reflects it back as natural. The map made the world and everything appears to correspond with it. Under such conditions, alien ideologies become more unreal than science fiction and stranger than hieroglyphs. The home ideology, by contrast, functions like an all-encompassing matrix. The map holds everybody captive because they live inside of it.

IDEOLOGIES AS MAGNETIC AND DISENCHANTED

Why do people fall so hard for ideology? Why are they capable of tearing up friendships and families, forming new communities, embarking on mass migrations, sacrificing wealth, suffering physically, or even spilling blood for these maps? After all, the history of ideology reveals lands littered with bodies. Every ideological map has at one time or another been drawn in the red ink of massacres.

The answer lies in the fact that ideologies are worldmaking and guide us at the largest scale. They are not outside of material reality but organize it – money, prizes, status, health and other goods. They also encompass loftier goals of justice, honour, recognition and even holiness. Whether wrongly or rightly, anything that we care about might be given space, or violently stamped out, by a given ideological programme. Likewise, even mundane emotions, desires, aspirations, and fears can be grafted into its matrix. Thus, the stakes of ideology are exceptionally high.

Ideology always proposes some vision of a good society with our life at its service. When one is attracted to an ideology there is an intense ethical *magnetism* to it. Indeed, many people fall for ideology similarly to falling in love or converting to a religion. This also suggests why suspending belief in one's own ideology (in order to listen to a rival) is so difficult. After all, is detaching in this way not a betrayal? Does it not threaten justice and unmoor one's sense of self? Ideologies come with their own missions, vocations, preachers, pastors and zealots.

At the same time, ideology's intense magnetism does not exclude the possibility that individuals can experience alienation or dry spells. As with religious faith, adherents can continue going through the motions without believing very intensely anymore. It is even possible to sit in the doorway of an ideology and strike an aloof, ironic pose, without actually leaving the building.[12] None of this changes – and, in fact, presupposes – the truth that ideologies radiate an intense magnetic pull.

Religions and ideologies share deep moral sources, but the similarity can also be overstated. After all, the world religions are millennia older than the major ideologies. In fact, our modern ideologies are the product of what the philosopher Charles Taylor calls a secular age, occurring in an "immanent frame".[13] When it comes to politics, Taylor has shown at length that people today self-consciously mobilize within immanent historical time. By contrast, many premodern people believed spirits, gods, and supernatural entities established and maintained their regimes, regardless of any human efforts. Such a view is expressed by the captain in Shakespeare's *Richard II* who reports seeing "signs" that "forerun the death of kings" including "withered" trees, "meteors" and the moon turned "bloody" red.[14] Sure enough, a few acts later, King Richard is dead.

By contrast, modern ideology (even when religious) self-consciously occurs inside historical time. Religious conservatives and traditionalists today do not expect the moon, trees and meteors to act or signal on behalf of their politics. Ideologies are in this specific sense *disenchanted* – mobilizing followers around programmes led by human, all-too-human efforts to get them off the ground. The pattern of politics typical of the French Revolution, with the theorizing of ideas and rallying behind them, is now universal. Granted, the liquidity of ideologies allows them to sometimes absorb and coopt an older religious tradition in its entirety. When this happens, religion continues to exist like the lost city of Atlantis, submerged at the bottom of an ideological ocean.

CHARTING A PATH FORWARD

Because ideologies are fraught with danger, many try to steer clear of them altogether. Such people believe themselves to be "non-ideological" and "not political". However, the attempt to escape ideology by this route is a false solution to a real problem. We cannot opt to be "ideology-free" because in doing so, we simply continue participating in the dominant ideologies without awareness. Modern society is itself a living artifact of various competing ideologies. To proclaim oneself beyond ideology is the surest sign that one is adrift in it.

Other people instead attempt to inoculate themselves against ideology by proclaiming they believe in nothing more than science, data and logic. Admittedly empirical facts and logic do exert some critical force over ideology (I shall sometimes draw on their authority in these pages). For example, science has an important role to play in establishing inconvenient facts that may contradict a particular ideology. Similarly, logicians can do damage to an ideology by diagnosing its inner inconsistencies.

Unfortunately, however, these approaches only take us so far in the realm of ideology. As I shall try to show, most of the major ideologies are not so easily defeated (or vindicated). This is because ideologies are visions of a good society that always go beyond the merely factual and logical to pose basic questions of meaning and significance. As such, they cannot be settled by empirical or logical claims alone. They instead require a broader conception of reason that includes the interpretive rationality of the storytelling disciplines. Part of settling ideological disputes involves deciphering the meaning or significance of political life. This is far from relativistic. We continually hold people accountable for stories that are interpretively inferior accounts of the meaning of something or else generate an ethically undesirable account. These are precisely the sorts of debates central to disciplines in the humanities like literature, religion, the arts and history.

For example, one important form of criticism I shall make of ideology that draws on these disciplines is the idea of self-narration. I shall argue time and again that a given ideology is inferior because it cannot tell its own story as cultural, instead claiming to somehow be natural, common-sensical, or scientific. Conversely, ideological variants from across different traditions that do not fall into this trap, can at least claim superiority to their rivals in this key regard. My account of ideology is therefore attentive to what followers of a given programme think, without falling into uncritical relativism. I shall draw on philosophical analysis, the natural sciences, and most of all the storytelling disciplines with their art of interpretation, to critique ideology. By the end, perhaps readers will have a clearer sense of what they find reasonable and ethically attractive in rival ideological maps.

Thus, we set out on our journey into ideology with an orienting philosophical compass. Ideologies are not simply the crazed beliefs of your political foes. They are cultural traditions; they are world-making maps; they are liquid, narrative and ethically magnetic visions. While ideologies share some similarities with religions they also belong to our disenchanted and modern age.

We begin from the context of the United States, not because it is universal, but because all cultural investigation must start from some location. My hope is, however, to move outward towards a more global vision. The first two chapters engage the ideologies of the American founding, including not only classical liberalism and civic republicanism but also white supremacy. The middle chapters explore the hyperpolarization of left and right including progressive liberalism, right libertarianism, conservatism, fascism, socialism and communism. The final cluster of chapters dives into ideologies that scramble the whole notion of a clean split between left versus right, such as nationalism, multiculturalism, feminism and ecologism. I conclude reflecting on what it means to live in an ideological age and how to argue about ideological differences in a way that is critical, objective and not reductive or dismissive.

While I do not offer a complete account of any one ideology, I do attempt to orient readers within the upheaval and tumult of the competing maps. No ideology comes out unscathed. Cultural awareness of ideologies highlights inner tensions and dilemmas – I call out all the ideological traditions whenever they claim the false status of nature or science. I also attempt to fairly identify their deeper moral sources and affirm why they can resonate so powerfully for their followers.

Although the book is meant to be read cover to cover, readers can also jump to those chapters treating ideologies that most interest them and which they hope to see illuminated and criticized by cultural interpretation. My hope is that the reader will fall slightly less in love with their own ideology, and have a more nuanced, if still critical understanding of one that is not their own. The failure to do so could leave us lost in a map so big it conceals the world.

PART I

Strange roots: early America

1

Liberal by nature: varieties of classical liberalism

Liberalism is a map whose recurring landmarks include: the establishment of individual rights, the formation of government based on a contract, equality before the law, the protection of private property, and an affirmation of religious and ethical tolerance. This map has at times appeared so utterly dominant in the United States as to create the illusion of being the country's lone ideology. As the political scientist Louis Hartz declared, "there has never been a 'liberal movement' or a real 'liberal party' in America: we have only had the American Way of Life".[1] According to Hartz, all major ideological conflict in the USA was an intramural debate between left-versus-right liberals, who might disagree over specific rights (say, the right to gun ownership or the right to healthcare) but never questioned the fundamental existence of individual rights as such. Indeed, even the country's leading poets echoed liberal ideas about the freedom to noninterference, teaching adages like "good fences make good neighbors".[2] And every American intuitively sensed that the best fences were not made of metal or solid board but of individual rights.

In this way, the United States was imagined as the land of liberalism, its ideological coordinates baked into the very canyons, forests, deserts and highways. Any ideology outside of liberalism's borders (say, socialism or fascism) was deemed un-American, an invasive species. Likewise, forms of racial hierarchy that seemingly flourished in the United States, were classified as anomalous and fringe. Hartz, for instance, suggested that racial hierarchy was mostly limited to the American South, which was the "alien child in a liberal family" that "after the Civil War . . . fell quickly into oblivion".[3]

Today no serious scholar of American politics accepts Hartz's breezy dismissal of the South or his attempt to expunge other regions of participation in racism. Instead, Hartz's thesis is interesting not as an empirical truth of social science, but as an artifact of liberal ideology itself. Although Hartz thought of himself as offering value-neutral descriptions of the political topography, he was instead unwittingly retracing and reinforcing the lines of an ideological map.

Hartz's mistake is instructive because it implies that in certain places – say, Harvard in the late twentieth century – an ideology can appear englobing. All the institutions, practices, rituals, beliefs and gestures seem saturated by its politics, forming into a kind of world. One is liberal in places like Cambridge, Massachusetts without even thinking twice about it. Liberalism is adopted in such communities not in theory first but as a lived out set of practices. One learns to behave like a good liberal – tolerating differences, respecting the press, pursuing self-reliance – and only much later (perhaps through education) one is astonished to learn that one is a "liberal". Under such conditions, liberalism might even assume the authority of mere decency, civility and good sense.

Add to this that major strains of classical liberal philosophy present themselves as natural, even scientific, and the illusion of the near inevitability of liberalism can become overwhelming. At least this is part of what I shall try to show in the case of two of classical liberalism's earliest manifestations: natural-rights theory and utilitarianism. Classical liberals frequently conceive of their politics not as one contestable culture among others, but as a kind of universal, global geography.

THE NEW WORLD OF LOCKEAN LIBERALISM

The dazzling revolutionary ascent of classical liberalism in the late eighteenth century was at least partly due to the potency of its vision. Here was a system of beliefs that not only laid bare the human condition but also offered a clear path to emancipation. This was not a politics draped in the murky metaphysics and theological opacities of the *ancien régime*. It was plainspoken, down-to-earth, even natural. In the words of the American Revolution's greatest promoter – Thomas Paine – liberal rights were "nothing more than simple facts, plain arguments, and commonsense".[4] The authors of the Declaration of Independence concurred: liberalism was "self-evident".

But how did an ideology virtually unknown a few generations earlier come to be hailed as the wisdom of the people and obvious to anyone who stopped to think rationally for a moment? One answer is found by returning to the theory of natural rights as articulated by John Locke. It was Locke's *Second Treatise of Government* that perhaps more than any other document in history helped later liberals envision their ideology as innate and primordial. After all, according to Locke, individual rights existed before all politics and were clearly discernible in the pure light of "natural reason" – or human thought free of special revelations and inherited traditions.[5]

Curiously, Europe's encounter with the "New World" played a key role in spurring Locke to his worldmaking act of the imagination. Many times in the *Second Treatise*, Locke suggests the natives of the Americas live in a "state of nature" or primordial condition of individual liberties and rights. In passages that would later be echoed by Hartz, Locke described the Americas as liberty's natural homeland (especially the northern expanses faraway from "the conquering swords, and spreading domination of the two great empires of Peru and Mexico").[6] "In many parts of America", Locke wrote, "there was not Government at all" and the natives "enjoyed their own natural freedom".[7] And "in the beginning all the world was America".[8]

For Locke, natural rights flourished whenever usurping governments, traditions and institutions were rolled back. Left to themselves, *Homo sapiens* were naturally and spontaneously liberal, asserting their individual rights, especially the right to property. Although Locke knew inhabitants of the state of nature would be unable to rehearse the philosophical arguments of the *Second Treatise*, he believed they would have a strong intuitive sense of the absolute ownership of their own body and the fruits of their labour. "Every man", Locke wrote, "has a property in his own person: this nobody has any right to but himself".[9] Nature was therefore a system coordinating self-owning individuals: a "state of perfect freedom" without being a lawless "state of license".[10]

Of course, Locke conceded that nature itself was originally in common. But he also reasoned that individual survival required carving out exclusive claims on food, water, shelter and other such goods. Thus, the rudiments of a right to individual private property were natural. While no person could take more than needed for subsistence, natural law also dictated that the fruit of one's labour was private. "He that is nourished by the acorns he picked", Locke explained, "appropriated them to himself. Nobody can deny but the nourishment is his".[11] Nature, therefore, furnished the basis for later governments to police and protect private property and with it the enclosure and sale of land.

Fatefully, these doctrines had a tight ideological fit with Europe's burgeoning project of settler colonialism in the Americas. Europeans using natural reason were no less in communion with the state of nature than the indigenous tribes. As for the land occupied by tribes of hunter-gatherers these were clearly unclaimed. Nature showed the "Indians" had only removed the game they hunted or wild fruit they picked. The land beneath it remained open to appropriation by mixing labour through enclosure and agricultural development.

Needless to say, the historical record does not support Locke's assertion that the state of nature existed among the peoples of North America (let alone as the universal, aboriginal condition of humankind). Instead, as already seen in the case of the Lenape, the Indigenous peoples of North America, facing massive waves of settlers, were frequently baffled by claims to individual land enclosure. As the Nez Perce leader, Chief Joseph, declared: "The country was made without lines of demarcation and it is no man's business to divide it".[12] The sentiment was echoed by the Lakota warrior, Crazy Horse: "One does not sell the earth upon which the people walk".[13] In such cultures, the land was communally inhabited. Carving up the continent into a grid of individual-use claims was unreasonable, perhaps even blasphemous.

In short, the true anthropological situation is nearly the exact opposite of Locke's state of nature. Humans are, in fact, spontaneously cultural creatures – for them culture is paradoxically natural. As Clifford Geertz put it: humans are "in physical terms an ... unfinished animal" only made whole "through culture".[14] This means "there is no such thing as a human nature independent of culture" and humans "would be unworkable monstrosities" and "mental basket cases" without it.[15] Locke's error was to believe he had reached the natural, bedrock society by subtracting culture; he never seems to have realized that no such thing exists.

Locke is, therefore, a paradigmatic case of a philosopher who lacks (ideological) self-knowledge. He unwittingly helped invent and promulgate the very thing he believed himself to be simply uncovering empirically. The more his map was enacted by mass mobilization, the more it appeared to be the simple, verifiable truth of the world. A newly born culture served the role of corroborating nature. Yet part of the very force of Lockean liberalism is that it naturalizes its own politics and therefore covers over its own original creative, even poetic act. The basic justifying concepts of later liberal-capitalism appear as part of the very machinery of the world. Liberal ideology is inescapable because it is natural. You can run to the farthest corner of the globe – to the final Alaskan frontier or the Hawaiian Islands – and liberalism will be there waiting to greet you.

Yet Locke's tremendous act of ideological creativity is not only forceful due to what it naturalizes, but also because of what it renders artificial. Most readers of the *Second Treatise* do not meditate enough on the astonishing list of features of human life rendered unnatural simply by not appearing in the Lockean state of nature. These include but are not exhausted by: community, revealed religion, the arts, kin networks, friendship, prolonged dialogue, customs, rituals, sports, group play, and on, and on. Of course, many of these very same items are vulnerable to erosion – albeit never fully disappearing – in highly individualistic versions of liberal society.[16] The subtractive powers of the Lockean vision are therefore capable of remaking the world in their image.

Like a master artist drawing negative space, Locke's positive picture nonetheless also emerges: a society of individual autonomy and market exchange where no one is coerced and everyone's rights are respected, their differences tolerated. The blunt simplicity and magnificent individual independence of this map carries a kind of magnetism or energy. Humans following its coordinates are confident about their rights and liberties. Free of the authority of governments, churches, customs, ancestors, and all such hierarchies, the individual can at last, in plainspoken language, claim basic ownership over his or her person. All of this, moreover, is accomplished through the immediate and self-evident power of simple reason and natural intuition.

LIVING INSIDE LOCKE

So confident can those guided by a Lockean map become in their natural independence that they hasten to leave any association (family, town, workplace, church, region, and even government) seen as encroaching on their autonomy. Lockean freedom consists in casting off the many attempts to usurp self-ownership. Everything from divorcing to changing jobs and leaving town, can take on the resonances of a primordial emancipatory act.

Similarly, the American fascination with the car and road trips is sometimes expressive of this ideological culture. Facing the highway or the wilderness solo – not in clans, communes, or even stable friendships – can be configured as an iconic act of independence. One can perceive its traces in everyone from Jack Kerouac and Bob Dylan (with their restless odes to the road) to Henry David Thoreau and Chris McCandless (trekking into the wilderness). Casting off community and exercising one's autonomy on the interstate or deep in nature, becomes not an act of hermetic asceticism or misanthropy, but an unmistakable political feat.

Since humans are meaning-making creatures, an ideology's picture of liberation can shape identity. Indeed, so ethically magnetic is the story woven by Locke that those most deeply in its thrall sometimes find themselves wondering why they should remain within society at all. Why not find a remote patch of nature and build a cabin there? Or, less dramatically, why not simply withdraw into one's own life inside the confines of a house or apartment? "The Soul selects her own Society", Emily Dickinson (who rarely left the house) exquisitely wrote, "then shuts the Door – to her divine Majority".[17]

Of course, all of this is only part of the story. Locke also offers compelling reasons for setting up a society of individuals coordinating markets and maintaining a government. Although nature includes rights and laws (even allowing for individual executive power to stand one's ground) there is, nonetheless, the unstable absence of a neutral judge between otherwise autonomous individuals. Government, then, in this key inspiration for later liberal ideology, is conceived as a neutral arbiter or referee. The focus of government is most certainly not to decide on the endless metaphysical and ethical controversies of religion and philosophy. Locke perhaps believed, not entirely unpersuasively, that many of these questions resisted final resolution by natural reason. Instead, in Lockean government, each individual is given the freedom to ponder over and decide metaphysical questions for themselves.

Again, there is a cultural force to the Lockean map: not meddling in a neighbour's own answer to basic existential questions is a sign of respect for their freedom and independence. Although it might sometimes fall into indifferentism or vulgar relativism, it can also encompass a high standard of the affirmation of human dignity. Indeed, part of the ongoing magnetism of Lockean ideology is the promise of a form of government that treats each person equally in terms of their right to self-ownership and the protection of their ability to decide for themselves what is a good life. Lockean-inspired liberalism is anti-paternalistic and promises a kind of universal adulthood based on the rational and independent exercise of one's own faculties.

Central to the achievement of this rightly ordered society is the Lockean image of a contract. Like the economic contracts of the market, government itself is set up in terms of explicitly codified agreements between parties each looking after their own interests. In the Lockean case, government is the arbiter and protector of individual rights. Loyalty to it is an expression of one's own rational desire for independence and the securing of basic material interests (especially the property of one's own person). In principle, the freedom of each works in contract for the preservation of the freedom of all.

However, unlike conventional contracts, Locke's contract is not signed by all members of society. Consent is implied. This involves what appears commonsensical inside the Lockean map, but which from the outside can seem strange: namely, a contract which one imagines having signed. The continual habituation to contracts in Lockean societies, through run-of-the-mill economic and legal transactions, helps individuals picture themselves as having signed – if only in invisible ink – the most fundamental contract of all. In the mind's eye, one can witness the founding members of a republic ritualistically signing the document as legal proxies for one's own assent (albeit decades and even centuries later).

This weirdest of contractual agreements is essential to the non-coercive principles of Lockean government. Imagining a primordial act of free consent is crucial to remaining ethically attached to such forms of government. If nature is imagined in Locke, so too is the most basic act in the formation of society. The original contract, in this way, in spite of all the talk of rationalism and economic interests, is in fact much closer to poetry and myth.

The primordial myth of a contract gives Lockeans their peculiar cultural perception that all relations are chosen and consensual. Even if not explicitly formulated into the legalese of a contract – say, as in the case of natural childbirth – all relations might later be absorbed into the coordinates of this juridical grid. Yes, there is a disenchanting effect that both conservatives and radicals alike have decried ever since (reducing all of society to mere contracts and interests!) but there is also a stirring implied notion of individual independence that can seize anybody who has ever dreamt of leaving a suffocating community behind and making a fresh start.

The famous "right to exit", both at the individual and societal level, is one of this ideology's most important features. Whether it is, in fact, economically and materially feasible – and very often it is not – it nonetheless plays an outsized role. This is because a contract one is born into, did not actually sign, and can never really leave, is not freely chosen in any meaningful sense. Classical liberalism thus sets the cultural pattern of the dream of a bigger horizon: "Get out of Dodge", leave home, or even commit to a life of endless rolling mobility. One must, in principle, be able to exit all possible relations. Lockean liberalism's enactment of contract and exit remain key landmarks on this ideological map and part of how its story is enacted. Truly millions live inside the world of this contract. It is a living narrative.

DO LOCKEANS LACK SOLIDARITY?

A host of unresolved tensions arise within natural-rights ideology, capable of taxing the minds of even its greatest theorists. One crucial line of questioning concerns whether a society of individuals endeavouring towards self-interested autonomy can really hold together? What if extreme hardship rolls around – war, economic depression, pandemics, natural disasters, or other such calamities? Will citizens habituated to a culture of separateness and individual calculation (mostly free of any consideration of the commons or cooperation on a public good) make the sacrifices necessary to help one another through the crisis? Or, on the contrary, will they become so intensely estranged and even hostile to one another that they are virtually incapable of social coordination and the very liberal order collapses?

Some of these questions, we shall see tackled with great ingenuity by later mutations in liberal ideology. But Locke's implied resolution to the problem of social solidarity was to posit a counterbalancing sentiment as checking the liberal tendency towards extreme individualism. So, for example, he suggested that in a state of nature, reason would set limits on the acquisition of goods and hording. Specifically, stockpiling beyond those things necessary for survival, without leaving enough for others to subsist, was a violation of the law of reason. Every person had a right to live; and, Locke wrote, "whatever is beyond this, is more than his share, and belongs to others".[18]

Adam Smith also tackled the problem of classical liberalism's unbounding of the individual as in tension with social demands for cooperation and common sacrifice. Smith's *The Theory of Moral Sentiments* argued that liberal society was held together not only by egoistic calculations but also "humane" sentiments of "pity or compassion" for the "misery of others". Such sociable sentiments were supposedly natural, spontaneously present in all humans to some degree, even the "most hardened violator of the laws". Indeed, their existence, according to Smith, was a "fact too obvious to require any instances to prove".[19]

These sociable sentiments softened liberal agents, motivating them to aid others in need. They also helped engender a culture of civility in which rather than driving the hardest bargain possible, a liberal would rather retain relatively nice relations with fellow citizens. A kind of ideological personality thus emerged from this cultural map: an individual who prized civility as a social lubricant on the otherwise harsh and grinding mechanics of individual competition and isolation. Liberals were predisposed to be "nice" – not heroically self-sacrificial but neither absolutely indifferent – as they brushed up against one another in markets and other public spaces.

This ideological culture also inspired sentiments of social empathy and humanitarian enthusiasm that favoured nondiscrimination on the basis of race, religion, ethnicity, sex, language, or other such differences. Instead, a cosmopolitan community might emerge coordinated by markets and human rights. In this way, the map remade the world – looking to expand the reign of tolerant, practical-minded individuals. The world's many civilizations could acquire the liberal disposition towards rational toleration, civility, and sentimental commitment to human dignity.

But here a deep tension also resurfaces: namely, if liberalism is a culture, then both its sentiments and rational calculations need to be learned. Contra both Locke and Smith, liberalism is not natural either across the vast expanses of the globe or internal to liberal society. The assumption that beneath the crust of inherited custom all humans are spontaneously liberal is false. What to do, then, if this ideology is either alien to an existent culture or else goes into steep decline in a once liberal polity?

If those committed to liberal politics attempt to impose an education inculcating liberal ways of thinking, civility, and tolerant speech, then this appears to violate the sovereign self-ownership of individual rights. Classical liberals often presume a common good – including the culture of liberalism itself – that they struggle to secure without violating their own principles. To escape this dilemma, classical liberals would need to learn to grasp their map as one among others. They would also need a significantly modified form of their ideology that is able to reconcile individual liberty to some protection of the commons against mass defection. To assume the commons is simply naturally or spontaneously secured is to fundamentally misunderstand ideologies as forms of meaning-making and not a kind of natural or inescapable social mechanics.

There is, then, an unresolved conflict in early liberalism, namely: are liberal agents to be discovered or do they need to be culturally cultivated and produced? This problem of culture did not occur to Locke, Smith, and their allies because they expected a liberalism of interests and sentiments to be innate to the human condition. They had naturalized their own ideology and remained captive to this mistaken view. It would require later developments in so-called progressive or social liberalism (which we shall explore in Chapter 3) to articulate possible resources for overcoming these difficult problems.

UTILITY AND NUMBER-CRUNCHING

A later wave of liberalism had no patience for state-of-nature speculations or arguments about the metaphysical permanence of rights. After all, on what plane of reality did rights exist? Could you see a right? Smell it? Pick it out with any of the senses? Certainly, there was nothing empirical about rights. As Jeremy Bentham, the founder of the ethical school on which a new wave of liberalism would be based, joked in one of the most famous barbs in the history of philosophy: "natural rights" were "nonsense upon stilts".[20]

Utilitarianism thus burst on the scene as a hard-nosed, unsentimental alternative. Its foundational claim – that ethics rested on the attempt to increase pleasure and diminish pain – was declared by Bentham as an indubitable finding of "moral science".[21] The "principle of utility" could be verified in the actions and "lives of men in general" who acted consistently in this manner "without thinking of it".[22] In other words, human beings were naturally and spontaneously hedonistic. Politically speaking, what was good or bad could be rationally calculated by tallying up the effects on overall pleasure (sometimes referred to as happiness or utility) for the greatest number of individuals. "Pleasure then, and the avoidance of pains", Bentham declared, "are the ends which the legislator has in view".[23]

The method Bentham developed for such massive cost–benefit analyses, which was later commonly referred to as *felicific calculus*, involved a complex attempt to quantify the social utility of actions. Bentham argued that in addition to considering the number of persons impacted by a policy, pleasure itself could be numerically quantified along such axes as intensity, duration, purity, and proximity. The model legislator was a coolheaded number-cruncher, processing the hard data of a policy science. Government action was to be determined through a combination of social forecasting and mathematics. After a political administrator had carefully forecast the consequences of an action, all that remained was to "sum up all the values of all the pleasures on the one side, and those of all the pains on the other" to arrive at a "moral judgment".[24]

Admittedly, Bentham's bizarre and ultimately unworkable system of *felicific calculus* is now a historical curiosity – one of so many discarded "sciences" of human behaviour. Whether any utilitarian ethic worthy of the name has survived the failure to quantify pleasure is a several-century-long dispute among philosophers.[25] What is certain, however, is that Bentham's more general ideological programme of rule via technocratic policy science is alive and well. A particularly influential strain of liberalism centres precisely on elites forging no-frills policy that claims for itself "non-partisan", scientific status over the well-being or welfare of the greatest number. Bentham's ideological children are those liberals – policy gurus, economists, administrators, public health experts, bureaucrats and managers – convinced that politics is resolvable through careful statistical analysis.

Ideologies, as worldmaking maps, create types of selves and do not simply describe reality. This was true of the earlier, natural rights form of liberalism, which made possible its own array of ideological characters (for example, the civil, tolerant, but also practical-minded liberal of interests and sentiments, often donning a costume of aristocratic, learned leisure and powdered wigs). Now utilitarianism also offered cultural resources for generating a new kind of liberal personality: the unsentimental technocrat, the matter-of-fact number-cruncher, and the studious policy wonk.

Utilitarianism's alternative culture of liberalism rejected the sentimental and rational gentlemen liberal of the Enlightenment. In its place was a highly managerial politics, concerned with cost–benefit analyses of various quantifiable social units. Of course, the calculative currencies circulating through the arteries of liberal-utilitarian ideology later changed in countless ways: no longer Benthamite units of pleasure but other supposedly more countable items like profits, carbon emissions, test scores, mortality rates, arrests, viral infections, and so on. The cultural persona behind the everchanging data sets remained the same: the engineering authority of the number-cruncher.

One deep moral attraction of this kind of ideological authority was a claim to scientific neutrality. Cost–benefit analyses might resolve for modern societies otherwise intractable social conflicts. "Let the numbers decide!" was a common ideological refrain. Not unlike Lockeanism, a bid was made on a form of power able to put the opaque disputes of religion and metaphysics into the past. Only here the framework of reason was derived from mathematization and the persuasive force of numbers. The utilitarian technocrat was increasingly ascendant in the restructuring of the major institutions of modern life: workplaces, schools, hospitals and governments. A massive project in world-building was inaugurated.

From the utilitarian perspective, for the first time in history, a fully scientific form of social organization was within grasp. Ideology could be put aside in favour of "science" and data. In addition, although utilitarianism typically took the form of top-down technocracy, it also contained dramatically egalitarian themes. Consider, for example, that on the utilitarian view individuals decided for themselves what counted as pleasurable. Sounding a liberal theme of individual autonomy: every person's pleasure was his or her own to decide. As a cultural map, utilitarian liberalism equalized what traditional morality had hierarchically arranged. In this way, moralists (both clerical and philosophical) were eclipsed by a new kind of managerial authority that allowed individuals to define for themselves what made them subjectively happy, while political authority limited itself to the objectivity of science and mathematics.

THE GENIUS OF UTILITY AND THE UTILITY OF GENIUS

Such links between utilitarianism and liberalism withstanding, there nonetheless remain serious philosophical tensions between the two. It is not difficult to see how starting from utilitarian premises one might arrive at illiberal conclusions that violate individual rights. For instance, what if a cultural majority in a given society experiences heightened utility by outlawing a minority's religious practices – for example, wearing the hijab or celebrating Mass? Utilitarianism's idea that an action is good based on its consequences for social well-being contradicts the belief that rights are intrinsically valuable and inviolable. The dilemma thus arises as to whether it is in principle permissible to violate liberal freedoms so long as enough people find it pleasurable to do so.

This is one way to understand the popular fascination with the trolley problem in recent years.[26] In this philosophical thought experiment, participants are asked to imagine a situation in which they must either intentionally divert a trolley car and kill one person or else take no action and allow the careening car to slaughter a large number of people. Interest in this philosophical chestnut may be expressive of deep anxieties internal to liberal ideology, which is routinely torn between the conflicting claims of rights and technocratic cost–benefit analyses.

After all, the fantasy of the trolley-car problem is arguably an all-too real conundrum for liberal politics wavering between stirring rhetoric about inviolable rights and cold calculations of collateral damage, moral hazard, scarce resources, market efficiencies, and the statistical sacrifice of individuals and groups. The truth is that political liberalism – in its mass-mobilized form – has never fully disentangled itself from the problem of both defending and dissolving individual rights in situations as heterogeneous as wars, healthcare, and economic recessions.

None of this is to say that liberalism lacks for valiant efforts to render these two opposing poles coherent. Most impressive so far – and the great genius of utilitarian philosophy – is John Stuart Mill. After all, it was Mill who opened up the possibility that liberal rights might be squared with utilitarian calculation. For Mill, this stemmed from the intuition that maximizing pleasure for the greatest number would ultimately require government to protect individual rights.

Mill's basic argumentative strategy was to claim that overall utility is served whenever society acts *as if* rights are in principle inviolable. In other words, individual rights are defensible not on intrinsic but consequentialist grounds. Many of these arguments are found in one of the great masterpieces of liberal ideology, *On Liberty*, published in 1859. For example, in what are now famous passages, Mill suggests that liberal rights secure nonconformism and, in doing so, increase societal happiness. This is partly derived from Mill's premise that "individuality" and pluralism are ineliminable features of the human species, such that "different experiments in living" are the best way to achieve overall "well-being".[27] But he also argued that a right to nonconformity increased utility in cases where the majority found a particular way of life disturbing or even morally objectionable.

Here Mill unleashed a battery of arguments including not only the possibility that nonconforming ways of life nurture geniuses that go on to benefit everyone with their inventions and innovations, but also that traditional morality itself might need to be enriched and expanded lest its "experience ... be too narrow" or not yet "interpreted ... rightly".[28] Genius, according to Mill, by definition broke out of conforming patterns of belief and practice. To put it somewhat playfully: the genius of liberalism was its ability to guard the freedom that made for geniuses. Liberal rights to nonconformity were not intrinsic and absolute but rather heightened social well-being by allowing for progress and innovation.

Of course, Mill conceded that many nonconformists were simply cranks and kooks. But he believed society had no way of eliminating all frauds without also snuffing out the geniuses. Besides, even self-destructive forms of nonconformity should be protected by individual rights (provided they did not harm others), as they remained of overall pedagogical value to society. Traditional morality could point to such cases as warnings and rational vindication of their own rules and customs. Likewise, the need to make the case for traditional morality in the face of such nonconformity assured that traditionalists did not adopt their own way of life in "ape-like ... imitation" but instead exercised their reason and agency.[29] Nonconformity, paradoxically, made for more vigorous and healthy traditionalists. Indeed, today's traditionalist might be tomorrow's nonconformist and vice versa.

In short, Mill advanced a brilliant defence of liberal rights as heightening the utility of seemingly opposing groups like traditionalists and avant-gardists as well as geniuses and cranks. This is one route to Mill's hugely influential articulation of individual rights as resting on the harm principle. As Mill wrote:

> The sole end for which mankind are warranted, individually or collectively, in interfering with the liberty of action of any of their number, is self-protection ... the only purpose for which power can be rightfully exercised over any member of a civilized community, against his will, is to prevent harm to others. His own good, either physical or moral is not a sufficient warrant.[30]

Mill's map of liberalism, therefore, did not simply tolerate differences but saw positive utility in nonconformity. For Mill, all of society benefited from those willing to stand out and risk being perceived as odd in order to follow their own conscience. This marks a dramatic ideological evolution of classical liberalism to not only absorb utilitarian principles but also romanticism's vision of genius as authentic and nonconforming.

SCIENCE OR RHETORIC?

Ideology is a map that does not simply describe but changes the world. Mill's writings are particularly suggestive of new identity possibilities within liberal ideology. We have seen that earlier liberalism already had inspired a range of characters. But possible ideological personas now expanded to include not only Bentham's technocrats but also starry-eyed dreamers, geniuses, misfits, nonconformists, as well as those who intentionally assumed the stance of provocateurs and polemicists. Shock liberalism was a tsunami-like cultural force unto itself – quite unlike the white-powdered wigs and gentlemanly civility of 1776.

Beholding the birth of such forms of liberal selfhood it is possible to see just how complex and rich Mill's blend of liberalism, romanticism and utilitarianism was. Of course, it is easy to call to mind the damaging or unstable cases of such personas (the demagogues, immoralists and crackpots) but the same culture has also inspired a range of virtuosos, experts and moral exemplars. And although Mill rests his case in *On Liberty* on utilitarian grounds, it is not at all clear that his vision of liberalism might not instead find support in alternative ethical, cultural, political, and even religious sources.

One problem with linking Mill's liberalism to his utilitarian philosophy is that the latter requires humans have the necessary knowledge to forecast outcomes for social utility. In other words, utilitarianism necessitates a strong form of social scientific prediction over the whole of society that continues to elude experts. A cultural view of ideology would expect to see this problem – after all, as creative meaning-makers, humans are not susceptible to impersonal scientific prediction.[31] But if a science of society is unavailable (either at present or perhaps ever) then Mill's arguments about individual liberty maximizing overall social utility are essentially rhetorical and not objective prognostications.

Utilitarian liberalism's problem with prediction – the unobtainability of a science of society – is ironically hidden by its own poetic and linguistic powers. Rhetorical appeals to data, numbers, and other cost–benefit analyses hide that this, too, is another cultural map and matrix of meanings. Indeed, even how happiness itself is experienced by individuals is not entirely independent of the cultural maps they use to guide them. A utilitarian political culture can produce people who have a utilitarian conception of their own pleasures and pains. The psychological theory that everyone is naturally hedonistic becomes looping and self-confirming. The Borgesian map has covered over reality as ideology crafts a world in its own image.

Once the map has engulfed the world in this way, gesturing at statistics and coolly observing that experts are simply following the maths or the data, can appear as the only scientific or rational way to organize society. Not unlike natural-rights liberalism, utilitarianism can lull its adherents into thinking a specific worldmaking map is an inescapable reality. Society then stops appearing as one possible culture among others, and reifies into a machine for fine-tuning. Its function is simply to maximize outputs, be those economic, psychological or social. When this happens, utilitarian cartography is mistaken for social geography.

Tellingly, the classical liberal tradition itself, far from reaching agreement over the one scientific or natural language for politics is itself splintered into rival cultures. The pressure stemming from these problems has inspired several dramatic mutations in liberal ideology (which must await development in Chapter 3). For now, a cultural conception of ideology helps us see that one can convert into liberal forms of selfhood just as surely as one can embody other ethical sources. That liberalism understands itself to be universal and rationalist does not spare it from being a cultural tradition that one must join – akin to joining a universalist religion like Christianity or Islam. By contrast, liberalism lost in its own map appears as the only scientific or rational way of being human. Oddly enough, to arrive at this place is to have become irrational about what is reasonable.

2

Other foundings: civic republicanism and White supremacy

The Lockean and Hartzian vision of North America as the primordial land of liberalism makes for a rapturous story. Yet as a historical narrative, it is no less mythological than the story of Romulus being suckled at the teat of a she-wolf. For better or worse, since before its founding, North America has been the site of clashing and rivalrous ideologies.

This chapter looks at two non-liberal maps that were present well before 1776. The first is a communal and participatory form of democracy – civic republicanism – that continues to inspire heterodox politics on both the left and the right. The second is a hierarchical racial politics – White supremacy – that erected several caste systems domestically and wove itself into later fascist movements across the globe.[1] Both of these ideologies continue to mix and blend in complex ways with other maps, including not only liberalism but also conservatism, nationalism, ecologism, and more. To fail to decode their symbols is to remain blind to the persistent ideological multiplicity of contemporary life.

THE FREEDOM OF CITIES

Civic republicanism might at first blush appear as an obscure ideological map whose territories have been heard of by only a few academics. But in truth, although a relatively small political tradition, civic republicanism has exercised an outsized influence in part by hybridizing with larger movements led by classical liberals, Greens, conservatives and socialists. It has left its mark, for example, on front-porch conservatives wishing to devolve power onto locality, as well as heterodox socialists who reject statism and wish for a democracy inspired by the Greek polis.

In North America, this ideology first took root in the Puritan townships of New England, with their fierce sense of independent self-rule. As the great theorist of civic republicanism – the French aristocrat Alexis de Tocqueville – put it in *Democracy in America*: "I can see the whole destiny of America contained in the first Puritan who landed on those shores".[2] Unlike natural-rights liberalism, civic republicans ascribe freedom not primarily to autonomous individuals but to the entire community and specifically cities. Such freedom is a cooperative accomplishment and not a natural, individualistic given.

This is what links modern civic republicanism to the classical political theories of ancient Greece, where liberty was often ascribed to the "polis". The classic republican city was neither a hulking metropolis nor spatially dispersed in the style of modern suburbs. Rather, it was big enough to sustain political independence, but also small enough to allow for the direct participation of all citizens in government. In this ideological map, an individual is only free insofar as he or she participates actively in a community that gives itself laws. A true democracy is participatory and deliberative, engaging each individual in self-rule. Arguably, by this demanding standard, the citizens of most liberal democracies (let alone other regimes) are not fully free.

The name *civic republican* is itself instructive for better understanding this ideology. "Civic" – derived from the Latin word for city – is also the basis for the word "citizen". For civic republicans the true citizen is not defined by passive legal status, much less by mere birth or ethnic belonging. Instead, a citizen is a kind of political agent who cares intensely about their city and is actively involved in taking turns ruling and being ruled. A city, in the civic republican sense, must not only have small enough assemblies for all to participate, but also economies that permit citizens the leisure to spend the hours necessary for public service. A life predominantly consumed by business or wages is not a free life. As Jean-Jacques Rousseau wrote describing the ethos of the cities of antiquity: "the word *finance* is a slave's word".[3]

The second word in this ideology's name is no less illuminating: republic or *res publica*, which in Latin means a public thing. Civic republicans see true cities as bounded by a shared experience that makes discerning a public or common good possible. They do not expect large-scale states or nations to successfully articulate a true notion of the common good because these do not allow for citizen participation and also lack a unity of experience within a limited locale. The common good of a community, according to civic republicans, is constituted by the particularity of a given historical, geographic and cultural context. What a city needs to thrive and remain free is often highly specific and does not apply to other cities let alone entire regions. Civic republicanism's recurrent demand that large-scale governments return power to cities is a direct result of these commitments.

How do such republican cities come into existence? To his credit, Tocqueville does not repeat Aristotle's mistake in *The Politics*, which asserts that the polis "belongs among the things that exist by nature".[4] Instead, throughout the pages of *Democracy in America*, Tocqueville presents civic republics as a historical and cultural phenomenon. The democratic freedom of cities emerges out of local cultures (for example, the particular Puritan ethos of the New England township). This implies that individuals wishing to advance this ideology must band together with their neighbours to nurture and build the right kind of civic culture from the ground up.

Indeed, the creation of tightly bound, personalistic, democratically-ruled cities is the central task of civic republicanism. Its highest goal is to raise up proud cities whose citizens rally to its laws and institutions as the object of their public affection. Ideologies, as worldmaking maps, can bring different sorts of political spaces into existence; in the modern world, non-republican cities include not only massive industrial metropolises but also rural villages, suburban bedroom communities, and various kinds of towns fully subordinate to the state. Civic republicanism is in competition with the ethos and ideologies of these rival forms of community. A true city, according to civic republicans, is a rare and precious thing.

LIBERALISM CONTRA LIBERTY

Tocqueville is also a vital source for the civic republican critique of individualistic liberalism. On this view, liberalism left unchecked is capable of destroying the freedom of cities. According to Tocqueville, this threat arises because classical liberalism can inspire an exaggerated sense of individual autonomy, in which people wrongly believe "their whole destiny is in their own hands".[5] When such an ideological culture becomes dominant, individuals increasingly cut themselves off from others and become atomized. Rather than cooperating with one another in democratic and associational experiments in self-rule, they withdraw into a circle of friends, family and acquaintances, abandoning wider society and "almost unaware of the fate of the rest".[6] Such persons come to believe they can resolve their problems alone. Politics itself, becomes an intrusion upon (and not the highest expression of) self-rule.

Far from viewing this relinquishment of society as a negation of liberty, classical liberalism instead encourages individuals to interpret such choices as justified by personal preferences. The result is that any sense of the commons becomes almost impossible to imagine. After all, civic republicans hold that individuals need a community to deliberate and grasp the public good. But to such isolated individuals everything in political life appears like a fight between self-interested factions; the "common good" is suddenly no more than rhetoric for limiting individual freedom.

More troubling still, civic republicans argue that individualistic atomization creates a corrosive sense of social desolation. The hollowing out of political life was a major worry not only for Tocqueville, but also later civic republicans like Robert Putnam who devised the haunting image of Americans gradually losing all community and "bowling alone".[7] Tocqueville speculated that such disconnected individuals were fertile ground for a new, modern kind of despotism, in which anonymous masses huddled around an increasingly hierarchical executive and administrative state.

Less drastically, a culture of disconnected individuals might reduce democracy to nothing more than periodic voting for representatives. For civic republicans, this could easily slide into oligarchic rule by a professional class of politicians selected via elections. Inevitably, this ruling class would be drawn from those with the economic means to carry out politics on a large scale. This is one reason why Tocqueville insisted rough material equality among citizens was a necessary condition for self-rule. Participation in politics, after all, required both the material surplus to turn one's attention away from the economy as well as the desire to pursue public and not solely private interests.

Once the hierarchies of the "free" market had become dominant, political decisions would primarily be made by elites horse-trading, logrolling and conducting other such negotiations. From within the civic republican map, the tendency of classical liberalism to depict politics as inescapably composed of competing interests – for example, as famously articulated in James Madison's *Federalist No. 10* – is the result of this ideology's inability to build communities with a true commons. Thus, for civic republicans, inequalities in both the private sector as well as in government, thwart the freedom of cities.

Part of the appeal of civic republicanism is its claim to offer a superior set of theories and practices for sustaining democratic participation and rule by the people than liberalism. If liberalism left unchecked by individualism leads to inequalities and the breakdown of the associations needed to create a democracy, then perhaps civic republicanism helps correct this tendency. Maybe liberalism can even be hybridized (as Tocqueville seems to have done) with the civic republican defence of cities. Yet devolving power onto locality has also come with its own unsettling tensions.

LOCAL TYRANNIES

Whatever one makes of Tocqueville's criticisms of classical liberal ideology, a cultural approach clarifies how behind words like "freedom", "democracy", "city", and "citizen" are lurking dramatically different meanings. Those unable to grasp civic republicanism's distinctive ideological vocabulary will also fail to appreciate the ethical magnetism this tradition exerts. For instance, affection for *cities* is a tremendously deep, if underrecognized, form of political attachment. Modern people – moving in liberalism's mass economic migrations – often fail to appreciate that this type of political affection even exists. Others have no experience of bounded communities of self-rule but instead live in sprawling urban and suburban spaces. Yet, as the case of Socrates' intense love of Athens shows, affection for cities is far older and more enduring than many modern objects of political allegiance.[8]

By envisioning a concrete locus of allegiance, civic republicanism also offers a solution to the problem of citizen identification that bedeviled classical liberalism. Where classical liberals struggle to attach self-interested individuals through a contract to a massive, abstract state, civic republicans instead propose a concrete loyalty to a home city. Presumably, deliberation and participation in a political community offers civic republicans a sense of common belonging and a shared project. In ideal cases, a virtuous cycle might form in which the more one participates and has a say in one's municipal government , the more this intensifies one's allegiance to it. Or, at least, this is one way this map might provide an ethically compelling vision to those recruited to its ranks.

Yet like other ideologies, civic republicanism also has pressure points. Such tensions do not immediately invalidate it, but can cause a crisis of faith and push people out of its orienting meanings in an experience not dissimilar to losing one's religion. A recurrent problem for civic republicanism is the tension between the ruling authority of the city and the possible violation of constituent members' citizenship and deliberative powers. For example, historically speaking, American localities have often been sites for violent exclusions of all sorts, including those of class, race, religion, gender, language, nationality, and myriad types of nonconformism. Civic self-rule can precisely become the place where individuals are denied any say in what their lives look like by either a minority that seizes control of city government or a majority that decides the "good" of the community demands such exclusions.

Part of how Tocqueville dealt with this problem was by blending the civic republican city with the liberal system of federalism. Stressing the devolution of power onto cities and towns, Tocqueville nonetheless nested these communities within a legal framework of federal rights as overarching rules for local experiments in self-rule. Yet once a federal government has the power to override locality in the name of rights, is not the independence of the city forfeited in favour of the individual liberal contract with the administrative state? If this is true, civic republicanism would resolve the dilemma only by morphing into a kind of de facto liberalism. Indeed, the fate of New England townships as a historical reality has arguably been just such a drift towards liberal politics and a loss of any robust or real civic independence. At the same time, a cultural approach could not hold that such developments were mechanistically fated or determined – the direction might instead be reversed towards a revival of cities and civic culture.

Critics of civic republicanism have also often questioned the viability of the freedom of cities in an age of enormous states wielding tremendous economic and military might. Is localism feasible as a rival to the Goliath of the state? Again, Tocqueville on the page seems to resolve this problem by hybridizing civic republicanism within a federal framework of liberalism. These and similar considerations help explain why it is not uncommon to hear Tocqueville classified as a species of liberal – a label he himself adopted in a heterodox way.[9] This would not mean that the conceptual and interpretive distinctions between civic republicanism and classical liberalism disappear. Rather, it would signal one path by which civic republicans have creatively modified their political culture. Liberalized civic republicanism, with all its tensions, might be more vitally alive than the project of reviving the pre-liberal polis.

Other ideologists have also made efforts at fusing larger traditions with the freedom of cities. Harvey Mansfield, for instance, has articulated a conservative civic republicanism that seeks to preserve tradition, while Robert Bellah grafted it onto a democratic socialism pursuing radically egalitarian localism.[10] Of course, no one familiar with American history needs to be told that local "freedom" can provide cover for racial caste. By this route, civic republicanism hybridizes with yet another ideological tradition to which we must now turn – White supremacy.

BUILDING RACIAL HIERARCHY

Referring to the experience of Black people in America, Malcolm X, famously declared: "We didn't land on Plymouth Rock... Plymouth Rock landed on us".[11] Part of the continuing power of Malcolm's well-known phrase is the deep perception that mapmaking (whether ideological or geographic) must involve choices not only of detail and scale, but also of perspective and significance. Where Tocqueville and Locke each in their own way saw North American history as defined by liberty, Malcolm instead draws attention to a land marred by violence and bondage. The continent was not stepped upon freely by millions of Black people, but lashed to their backs as a weight to carry.

Malcolm's inversion of who or what lands on the North American continent is a linguistic opening by which we might step out of the dominant ideological narratives and recognize the existence of other political realities. In fact, no less central a document than the United States Constitution remains unintelligible if one lacks familiarity with White supremacist ideology. After all, Article 1, Section 2, Clause 3 contains the infamous proclamation that Black slaves, while denied the right to vote, count as "three fifths" of a person when assigning members to the House of Representatives.

Beyond the cynical ploy to boost the power of Southern states in Congress, there is the more fundamental issue of the kind of ideological thinking that renders this clause intelligible in the first place. Why does the founding legal document of a purportedly liberal regime – drafted by "enlightened" rationalists – imagine Black people as only three fifths of a person and not a whole? Is not political liberalism premised on the axiom that each individual counts equally before the law as one? And to what extent, if any, does race even properly exist in a Lockean state of nature or in a utilitarian calculus of social well-being?

What is clear is that the fractionalizing of Black people in the US Constitution reflects a distinct political culture of racial hierarchy. As part of this, it is important to understand that White supremacist ideology is not accidentally associated with the rationalism and scientism of the Enlightenment, but represents a possible rival mutation and abuse of its authority. For, while modern racism avails itself of all kinds of cultural resources (including theology, myth and history), it nonetheless remains true that its dominant strains allege a "science" of racial biology (albeit one long since proved bogus by actual scientists).

Consider that modern White supremacy's central concept of a "race" is itself presented as a supposedly empirical fact of scientific classification. Later White supremacists have drawn on developments in evolution and genetics to claim that the human race is divisible into racial sub-types that exhibit superiority and inferiority in key capacities. The taxonomy of White supremacy is, of course, never meant to simply describe but enact an agenda of racial power and domination. In this way, scientism itself becomes a kind of ideological power – claiming that the only "rational" way to organize society is into a hierarchy of colour.

An early form of this scientistic ideology was advanced by no less a figure of Enlightenment rationalism than Thomas Jefferson. Jefferson was not only an original drafter of the Declaration of Independence but also a man Tocqueville anointed as "the most powerful apostle of democracy there has ever been".[12] Yet in a number of his writings, Jefferson suggested that Black and White people should be understood as "different species of the same genus" with differing "endowments both of body and mind".[13] Classification of the human race was possible, Jefferson claimed, due to observable "physical distinctions" such as "color, figure, and hair" that could be reductively associated with higher-order capacities like intelligence, emotional sophistication, sociability and artistic creativity.[14]

In Jefferson's taxonomy "whites" were supreme and various other races were subordinate with "blacks" located in the position of greatest inferiority. Black people, Jefferson asserted, required "less sleep", than whites and were also "more tolerant of heat", helped by "glands of the skin" that gave them a "strong and disagreeable odor".[15] Jefferson also postulated that Black people's "griefs" were more "transient", their "reason much inferior" and their "imagination ... dull, tasteless, and anomalous".[16] Although Jefferson admitted he was unsure of the cause of such differences, he was nonetheless convinced they were "fixed in nature" and "as real as if its seat and cause were better known to us".[17]

A cultural approach to ideology makes clear how Jefferson's pseudoscientific speculations remain naïve to the ability of ideological maps to create a world in their own image. It never occurs to Jefferson that rather than merely reporting the facts of nature, he is instead naturalizing the cultural particularities of White supremacy in his own society. Indeed, he is quite clearly justifying in theory what was already occurring around him in practice, offering as empirically true claims that even many of today's White supremacists would not advance. In doing so, Jefferson is not discovering the factual basis of race but helping create it as a sociopolitical category. After all, it is not difficult to detect in such absurd hypotheses as Black people smelling more, enduring greater heat, and feeling less sadness, a politics in which White plantation masters (like Jefferson himself) could drive their slaves with impunity, even to the point of death. What Jefferson observed as verifiable "science" was the product of White supremacist culture.

In fact, White supremacy is a paradigmatic case of an ideology that thinks it is making scientific distinctions, when it is in fact involved in constructing a political culture. Jefferson's clunky race "science" is a forerunner to more methodologically subtle theories like those of Charles Murray, Richard Herrnstein, James Q. Wilson, and countless others who self-stylize as hardnosed empiricists while committing the same basic blunder.[18] That blunder is to stipulate racialized natural types and let the differences created by a White supremacist organization of society count as the raw "data" proving racial hierarchy. In this way, the descriptive theories reinforce the very political reality that allows the observations to appear as factual in the first place.[19]

But the merely "empirically" given can, in fact, be the product of a generations-long project in ideological worldmaking. When this happens, a closed loop is formed in which White supremacy becomes evidence for its own reasonableness. The Borgesian map conceals the world. White supremacists betray their basic ideological befuddlement with the pathos they express before the need to constantly construct and police a hierarchy that is purportedly given by nature. They vacillate between supposedly cold claims to an obvious "science" and attempts to rally people into a way of life that is continually slipping out of their hands. The "natural" descriptions of White supremacy are, in fact, hidden worldbuilding commands.

RACISM'S HOOK

Given the inadequacy of White supremacy – both in its pretensions to "science" and as an ideology unable to account for its own cultural features – why does it continue to hook so many people? After all, a map that routinely fails to orient its followers is not worth very much. And yet, White supremacy not only has shaped the country's history, it continues to exercise influence on a global scale.

One answer is that White supremacy appears plausible to some people because it has made a bid at forcing the world into its patterns and hierarchies. While perhaps fewer people than a century ago explicitly avow White supremacist beliefs, we continue to live in a world concretely shaped by its legacies. This is tragic because it implies that White supremacy has a kind of terrible inertia and is to some degree adopted even by those who reject it but continue to live in spaces marked by its colour lines. For example, that class and race track each other so tightly in many countries is not some kind of unfortunate accident but a direct consequence of centuries of implementing racial hierarchy.

At a deeper level, White supremacy preys on a desire for self-assertion and domination over others. As James Baldwin arrestingly put it: "the reason people think it's important to be white is that they think it's important not to be black". He went on to elaborate: "they think it's important to be white because white means you are civilized, and being black means you are not civilized".[20] Baldwin is revealing something crucial about White supremacy's magnetism. Since whiteness is too broad a category to carry sociological content, consisting as it does of many rival cultures (English, Irish, Icelandic, Belgian, and so on) it is in fact only made manifest in relationship to the creation of blackness and other such racial categories. It is not an exaggeration to say that without the invention of the category "Black" there would be no category "White". White in a very real sense exists to negate and exercise power over "Black" and various browner, redder, or yellower others.

Baldwin also helps us see how people might be pulled into the ideological map of White supremacy in an effort to restore or assert their own sense of worth. They may fear their own lives are inferior or somehow lesser. White supremacy then offers a story: they may not be Shakespeare or Mozart or Napoleon, but they purportedly participate a little bit in that greatness by sharing blood, genetics, and whiteness with them. Baldwin saw that one allure of White supremacy is created precisely by the fear of being "Black" (this time not a purported biological category, but as an inferior social and political standing). Baldwin brilliantly suggests the resolution to the apparent paradox: individuals become White supremacists not because they discover they are White but in order to *become* White.

If society is already organized in various ways to economically and politically subordinate non-Whites, then White supremacy also grants access to a system of social and material privileges. Depending on the context, there are often very real bribes, both economic and political, offered to individuals and groups willing to reconfigure their cultural identities and join a self-designating "White" bloc over and against browner others. For example, White supremacy asks an Italian Catholic immigrant in the tri-state area to forget the many more differences he or she has with an Anglo-evangelical in the rural South, than with their Brown or Black neighbour in the same building. Colour becomes highest and overrides all else. Individuals are invited to support a colour system that secures a higher spot on the economic, political, social, and cultural pecking order. The hierarchy is then defended with fear and violence.

THE MANY FACES OF WHITE SUPREMACY

Once White supremacy's matrix of meanings is in place, it is capable of swallowing much of the perceptual field. As a cultural map it enacts a system of politics – producing "White", "Black", "Brown", "Yellow", and other such identities. This relies not simply on abstract theories, but a kind of magnetism or call to build a certain social reality. It is very important to remember that it was not lack of intelligence that made Jefferson a White supremacist, but rather a temptation to power and an exaltation of his own status as a superlatively rational (White) man of enlightened letters and science.

While openly White supremacist types of world-building and mobilization continue to play an active role in contemporary politics, this ideology has also devised more hidden forms. The meanings of racial caste are now often encoded into ideological languages that appear on the surface to have nothing to do with race at all. A key figure in this regard is John Calhoun – the antebellum American vice president and senator.

Like Jefferson, Calhoun fancied himself a man of the rational Enlightenment, a project he saw as compatible with subjugating Black people to a system of chattel slavery. As he stated in a speech to Congress in 1837: slavery was "a positive good" due to the "physical differences, as well as intellectual" between Black and White people.[21] In contrast to Tocqueville, Calhoun envisioned Southern plantations, not New England townships, as the rejuvenating heart of American politics. This was due to his conviction that the Constitution required a ruling class to carry out legislation. Chattel slavery, for Calhoun, sustained the leisure needed for self-government. Thus, in his ideological map, Madisonian, elite representatives were ideally agrarian slaveholders and not men preoccupied, as in the North, by capitalist markets. Paradoxically, the plantation became the sociological and material basis for liberal "freedom".

Of course, chattel slavery was itself a hybridization of White supremacy with markets: Black slaves extracted like raw "resources" from Africa were then bought and sold in a system of contracts in the Americas. Ideological practices of this kind often spoke the language of a right to ownership, with the strange contradiction that an entire group of people had been stripped of any such right for themselves. Within this context, Calhoun's ideological innovation – which remains a pervasive strategy for White supremacy – was to pivot away from explicit defences of racial domination and instead install colourblind rules whose result was still hierarchy. For example, Calhoun was an important source of the argument that the conflict between the North and South was a dispute over state versus federal rights and not the abolition of slavery. The Civil War has been recoded ever since by millions of people as a colourblind war over state's rights. In fact, it was precisely over state's rights to conduct chattel slavery.[22]

Perhaps Calhoun's most theoretically elaborate defence of White supremacy was his attempt to introduce the notion of "concurrent majorities" into liberal institutional design. Claiming he had discovered a "Science of Government", Calhoun's basic argument was that key minority constituencies were entitled to veto power over majority legislation.[23] As he put it, "each interest or portion of the community" constituted "its own majority" or "a concurrent voice in making and executing the laws".[24]

On the page, Calhoun's concurrent majorities were not defined in terms of privileging White people over Black people. Instead, the concept was presented as a neutral "science" of rational institutional design akin to James Madison's *Federalist Papers*. Yet White supremacy unmistakably entered the equation in terms of which minority groups were granted veto power over a majority. Should Black people as a bloc be given such a prerogative? After all, Calhoun wrote "every interest will be truly and fully represented", including all the "different interests, orders, classes, or portions into which a community may be divided".[25] Without openly avowing White supremacy, the tacit assumption was White plantation owners would wield the veto, while others, notably Black people, would not.

Calhoun's strategy of retaining racial supremacy by selectively applying supposedly neutral rules remains alive today. Arguably voter suppression and gerrymandering deploy a similar tactic. In such cases, race is not mentioned but the result is White minority dominance over Black and Brown constituencies. Another example is offered by the "War on Drugs", in which racial minorities are policed and sentenced in far higher numbers than White people for similar rates of illegal-substance violations. This higher percentage of policing and punishment drags millions of Black and Brown men into a system of mass-incarceration that has the effect of dramatically diminishing their civic and economic status.[26]

All this implies that outside Klu Klux Klan and neo-Nazi rallies, one should not always expect to hear White supremacy openly voiced. Instead, for centuries this ideology has fused with other maps – liberalism, civic republicanism, conservatism, nationalism, and so on. The cartographic lines of White supremacy are often drawn in an invisible ink that nonetheless results in a world organized according to colour. For this reason, declaring oneself "liberal" or "civic republican" or any other ideology is never a blanket inoculation against racist politics. Because ideologies are worldmaking, one might also not consciously hold any racist beliefs but continue to participate in social spaces and patterns of life whose arrangements are racialized. Meanings can always intermix. White supremacy's face keeps changing.

PART II

Polarizations: the left and the right

3

Dueling liberalisms: progressives versus right libertarians

Today it has again become fashionable to declare liberalism "failed" and totally sapped as a political culture. But ideologies are like rivers. They remain constant by continually swirling and changing. In the modern world, the major ideologies rarely if ever dry up, but instead pick new paths as they churn and mix with other cultural streams, rolling down the canyons, deltas and plains of history. For this reason, no human observer is able to predict with certainty an ideology's demise. Ideologies are, by their very nature, renewable.

One might suspect from reading the first chapter on classical liberalism that this tradition is done and dusted. But the truth is liberalism has never gone away. To the contrary, it is one of the most powerful political cultures shaping the modern world. It also continues to be a common, although by no means exclusive, ideological basis for capitalism. True, liberal-capitalism has experienced many dramatic crises, and sometimes teetered on the brink of collapse. But rather than disappearing, this complex conglomerate of meanings, practices, institutions, patterns of action, and regimes, has shown a tremendous ability to evolve and reinvent itself.

This chapter turns to liberalism one final time to examine how this massive tradition underwent two earthshaking transformations in the twentieth century that helped create a fierce polarization between left-versus-right variants. So strong is the division internal to contemporary liberalism that the two factions are often on friendlier terms with those outside their own tradition than with the opposing wing of their own ideology.

THE PROGRESSIVE CASE FOR POSITIVE RIGHTS

The left variant of liberalism is often referred to as "progressive" to underscore its conviction that liberal politics ought to be actively involved in evolving through history in order to more deeply realize individual freedom. Progressivism is also sometimes called "social liberalism" to signal its attempt to reform classical liberalism's atomistic streak. As a cultural map, this ideology pursues individual liberty, but in a way that experiments with new practices and allows for communal cooperation and a greater role for government.

To be sure, progressivism's departure from classical liberalism can be overstated. It inherits from this older tradition a number of key themes, including: the authority of natural reason; the affirmation of pluralism; the separation of church and state; the need for liberties of press, association, individual expression, and personal property. However, progressives are also sharply critical of earlier liberalism. Specifically, they believe that classical liberals are guilty of various excesses and exclusions that render their politics both unstable and less emancipatory than first meets the eye. Classical liberalism, in order to avoid becoming a force for domination and unfreedom, must be reformed.

One central way progressives see classical liberal ideology as defective is its idea of individual liberty. Readers will recall that both Locke's state of nature and Mill's "harm principle", define freedom as non-interference. Individuals are free so long as they are left alone in their private lives. When external constraints have been removed, humans are naturally and spontaneously autonomous. By contrast, the early theorists of progressive ideology rejected this laissez-faire notion of freedom arguing instead that individual liberty required securing certain communal goods of well-being (or "welfare" as it came to be popularly called). Individuals who lacked constraints but did not have the guarantee of a certain basic level of well-being or economic security were not necessarily free.

An important figure for advancing this line of thought was the British idealist, T. H. Green. In the late nineteenth century, Green argued that classical liberal "freedom of contract" was faulty because it neglected the social conditions necessary for individuals to meaningfully enter into free relations with one another.[1] Of course, classical liberals generally accepted that coercion was incompatible with the freedom of contract – for example, a signature obtained at gunpoint was null and void. But one of Green's insights was to dissect how classical liberalism was often blind to complex forms of coercion embodied in social and economic reality.

Specifically, individuals without a right to certain basic goods could be tacitly intimidated into unfavourable contracts by the threat of hunger, loss of medical care, housing, or other such privations should an offer of employment be refused. Individuals in liberal-capitalist markets who lacked a right to nutritional subsistence, housing, and healthcare were not autonomous but subject to a subtle and very real form of coercion. Similarly, a worker without a basic right to education (not only literacy and numeracy, but a civic understanding of rights) might be easily manipulated by wealthier and more well-educated parties to a contract. Freedom of contract required the substantive exercise of certain capacities, and not merely the removal of constraints. In other words, economic insecurity could be a subtle but very real and looming form of coercion into contract.

What the classical liberal map depicted as a simple exchange on a labour market was, upon closer inspection, subject to myriad forms of threat and duress. In the ideological worlds enacted by the classical liberal map – where the poor were in asymmetrical positions vis-à-vis the rich – inequality would continue to increase over a long series of contracts that compounded the initial disadvantage. Thus, steep inequality and the reassertion of inherited wealth in liberal-capitalist societies, was partly the result of a defective idea of freedom. On paper everyone was free, signing on the dotted line, but in reality, entire groups of people were under unrelenting stress to do jobs out of economic desperation.

Green's resolution was not to abolish liberal-capitalist markets and freedom of contract. Rather, rights to individual non-interference needed to be supplemented with rights to economic security or welfare that ensured certain capacities. This opened the door to a role for government in maintaining a baseline level of welfare (what is often colloquially referred to in progressive political culture as a "safety net") as a condition and not contradiction of liberal freedom. As Green put it, the role of government was to "maintain the conditions without which a free exercise of human faculties is impossible".[2] Such reforms, progressives believe, when judiciously enacted, would render liberal-capitalist societies more equitable, stable and free.

This is one way to understand why progressives call for positive rights and envision a true liberal society as one of a basic level of well-being. Progressives do not see these as a violation of classical liberal freedoms but as a necessary background set of conditions for their actualization. Failure to secure this expanded set of rights, leaving everything to laissez-faire markets, leads to self-defeating outcomes that paradoxically undermine individual autonomy. Indeed, a similar point could be made about the progressive crusade to live free of the fear of violent death by a firearm, and its clash with the classical liberal notion of the autonomous right to bear arms. For progressives, flawed assumptions of autonomy as natural and atomistic, lead to situations in which large swaths of society have their agency and sometimes their very lives negated in the name of some other person's "freedom".

IMAGINING FUTURE FREEDOMS

Green's writings provide one framework for interpreting the massive transformation of liberal democracies over the last century. In the United States, a progressive ideological map led to the construction of the New Deal welfare state as well as a political culture emphasizing social solidarity. Social liberals often attempt to replace the traditional language of self-interested individualism and factions, with a liberalism of common dreams and a "Great Society".

According to this map, much of the New Deal programme of universal well-being remains in the realm of the future. For example, Franklin Delano Roosevelt in a speech to Congress from 1944, called for an "economic bill of rights" to supplement the Constitution's original list of liberal rights. As part of this, Roosevelt proposed legal guarantees to housing, food, medical care, education, social security and employment.[3] The codification of such rights has remained a point of destination on the outer horizon of the progressive map ever since.

Progressivism is ethically animated by visions of a liberal

democracy that better fulfills classical liberalism's initial promise of individual liberty, pluralism and equality. This imaginative power is evident, for example, in the novels of John Steinbeck whose works, such as *The Grapes of Wrath*, often reveal the limitations of a liberalism that does not evolve into a more complete form of freedom.[4] It is likewise perceptible as the ideology of the folksongs of the early Bob Dylan or the popular music of Bruce Springsteen. Part of what draws millions of people to progressive politics is its perception that liberalism is not simply a set of accomplishments to be defended but a potential to be strived for and realized. A spirit of solidarity must be ever renewed and expanded.

Dreams of human emancipation are, of course, among the deepest moral sources of modern politics more generally. But progressive ideology also places a distinctive stress on the need for cultural innovation and avant-gardism. Government and the institutions of the state are far from the sole focus of progressive liberalism, which looks to reform beliefs and practices across society including, education, the arts, religion and spirituality, economy, and even diet and "wellness". In short, progressivism is an ethos and not merely an abstract policy agenda limited to economics.

A canonical expression of progressivism's experimental ethos was offered by the American pragmatist, John Dewey, in his 1934 essay "The Future of Liberalism". There Dewey called for an evolution away from "earlier liberalism" that recognized the "significance of individuality with respect to social policies alters with change of the conditions in which individuals live".[5] For Dewey, liberalism was centred on the question: What is required for individuals to be free today? Progressive ideology was in this way saturated by the distinctly modern awareness that the present is a break from the past and demands a novel response.

For this reason, progressives seek to innovate on social and political life in a potentially unlimited range of areas that go beyond the New Deal, such as: security (what counts as a gun today?); ecology (what is a healthy environment?); psychology (what is a healthy sexual ethics?), and so on. An enormously important area of progressive politics, that receives greater attention in Chapters 8 and 9, is its hybridization with romantic themes not only of ecological preservation but also individual authenticity in sexual politics, later encompassing feminism and LGBT. In terms of the latter, Mill's idea of a liberalism that positively affirms diversity and nonconformity fits within progressivism's commitment to emancipatory experimentation.

Paradoxically, on this view, liberalism only remains itself by imagining new possibilities. Because social and historical circumstances ceaselessly modify, so too do the ideological demands that guarantee individual freedom. Those who remain at a defence of the original rights to, say, limited government or a right to bear arms, end up paradoxically becoming the enemies to individual emancipation. Likewise, conservatives who resist social experimentation and change, stifle the innovation needed to emancipate individuals in the face of new problems. Progressive affinity with avant-gardism in music, painting, literature, fashion, religion, alternative diets, holistic medicine, narcotics, and wellness, are part of this wider political ethos of ceaseless modernization.

IS HISTORY LINEAR?

But what of progressivism's ability to accommodate the insight that ideologies are cultural? To their philosophical credit, theorists like Green and Dewey do not present politics as outside of culture and history. In this respect, they avoid the mistake of rendering liberalism as naturally primordial and ahistorical as occurred with Locke. Nonetheless, progressivism runs afoul of the cultural conception of ideology whenever it assumes that politics is developmentally linear. Indeed, the name "progressive" itself can sometimes mystify its adherents by implying that politics has a single resolution for all rational people and sooner or later arcs towards one political-ethical standpoint.

Progressives become lost in ideology whenever they expect that everyone will, by sheer dint of historical development or natural reason, become progressives like them. Not unlike earlier classical liberals, progressives at times interpret their ideology as obvious, self-evident, or commonsensical. When this happens, progressivism does not seem to be a contestable cultural map and form of world-making. Instead, it appears as the inescapable future geography of the entire globe. Becoming disoriented in this way leads to great frustrations in progressive politics. In some cases, it creates a situation in which progressives view anyone who does not subscribe to their ideology as either cognitively inferior or morally perverse. With this line of reasoning, if you are not a progressive you are either an idiot or wicked. You may also simply be a walking anachronism, whose days are numbered. Progressive ideology becomes completely synonymous with modernization. Not only every person, but every country on the planet, is tacitly expected to one day follow in the same ideological footsteps. Liberal progressives become the pinnacle and final point of human development.

But this is a confusion. There is no simple way for humans to converge rationally on a single ideological tradition because ideology is never about mere rationality, scientific analysis, or a commonsense moral code. Rather, ideologies offer rival visions of meaning and significance that can resonate in complex and different ways with particular human beings and their stories. No ideology is akin to a rational proof and this expectation is sure to lead to tremendous disappointments and perplexity in anyone who adopts it. Progressives who fall into this groove of thinking might ironically slide towards illiberal politics in a gambit to prod their fellow citizens into becoming the future selves they are already bound by history to be. Likewise, depression, disappointment, misanthropy and cynicism can overtake those who in their youth expect progressive politics to advance inexorably, only to discover that other ideologies (e.g., conservatism, communism, ethnic nationalism, fascism) have come roaring back instead.

This is not to say all progressives ascribe to this faulty developmental view of history. Indeed, Dewey's notion of pragmatically posing the question of individual freedom does not logically require a linear theory of modernization. Likewise, the evolution of the liberal notion of freedom by the likes of Green partly draws its force by claiming to fulfill the liberal tradition better than liberalism itself does. In other words, its claim is to internal progress within the liberal tradition and not to some arrow of history by which everyone inevitably becomes progressive if they only think properly.

Whatever flaws Green's or Dewey's respective theories might have, such an approach to ideology is certainly more philosophically formidable. Thus, progressive politics remains among a few of the most dynamic sources of ideological energy and mobilization in the modern world. Other types of liberals – as well as those outside the liberal tradition – will hardly understand the politics of their own time if they fail to grapple with it.

THE BACKLASH OF A "NEW LIBERALISM"

A new kind of right libertarianism was born in the late twentieth century as a direct rejection of progressivism, setting for itself the agenda of eliminating the welfare state, reasserting laissez-faire markets, and restoring freedom as individual non-interference. University of Chicago economist, Milton Friedman, suggested that the chief aim of this ideology was a return to the liberalism of the "late eighteenth and early nineteenth centuries".[6] But he also recognized that recuperating classical liberalism in the wake of progressivism's dramatic evolution required a "new liberalism".[7] In his 1951 essay, "Neo-Liberalism and Its Prospects", Friedman wrote that "neo-liberalism would accept the nineteenth-century liberal emphasis in the fundamental importance of the individual, but it would substitute for the nineteenth-century goal of laissez-faire as a means to this end, the goal of the competitive order".[8]

Those who follow what Friedman called a "neoliberal" map often instead self-apply names like "classical liberal", right "libertarian", or "conservative". The sharp differences between conservatism and this new liberalism – as well as attempts to reconcile the two – will be explored in Chapter 4. For now, it is important to note that libertarian ideas of individual autonomy are often adopted by progressives against traditional morality (as in the cases of gay marriage and abortion) or in campaigns to legalize narcotics or roll back the state's policing and military functions.

By contrast, neoliberalism advances a species of right-wing libertarianism that asserts individual autonomy and anti-statism but targeted at the realms of economics and wealth distribution. Although often unstated, such neoliberals or right libertarians assume that to survive in the competitive world of markets, individuals and families are best served by moralities of personal responsibility, frugality, sobriety and self-control. Followers of this map, therefore, are far less likely to support the liberalization of morality. They are likewise more prone to ally with conservatives in championing law-and-order deployments of the state (most notably the police and military) to defend private property both domestically and abroad. In all these ways they reject a libertarianism of the left, whose focus is often individual non-conformity and movement away from tradition. As Friedman emphasized, this species of right-wing libertarianism would be able to "expand a bit on the functions that would be exercised by the state" over classical liberalism, particularly in "the function of maintaining law and order".[9]

Of course, individuals can always mix and match their ideological beliefs in ways that deviate from a standard map. Ideologies are meanings and offer infinite possibilities for unique fusions – not unlike cuisines (think of, say, Tex-Mex) or musical genres (think of, blues and country). Individuals can and do meld progressive stances on narcotics, sexual ethics, and so on, with right libertarian views of economy. But more often than not, right libertarianism has not taken this form. And, in any case, enumerating every ideological possibility is neither feasible nor desirable, but akin to counting grains of sand.

The name "classical liberal" (which is sometimes adopted by followers of this ideology) can also be misleading. For, while right libertarians can legitimately claim common ancestry with earlier liberalism, they also developed a dramatically new political cartography. Indeed, the intense rivalry between progressives and right libertarians is partly due to the fact that each shares some kinship with the classical liberal past. This point needs a little explaining.

We already saw that classical liberalism taught that an enlightened polity would be held together through a combination of egoistic, contractual interests as well as sociable, altruistic sentiments. No less than Adam Smith (whose famous theory of markets as guided by an "invisible hand" is central to classical liberalism) believed that a society organized by economic calculation alone would collapse if not balanced by benevolent moral feelings. What liberalism needed was "fellow feeling" or an un-egoistic and cosmopolitan concern with "every man, merely because he is our fellow creature".[10]

The enlightened statesperson of 1776 was, therefore, an individual of leisure and erudition able to bracket self-interest and pursue the public good. This is why leaders and luminaries of the American Revolution were often suspicious of public office being held by those still engaged in private business. Such men, they believed, would be narrowly self-interested and unable to cultivate benevolent and humanitarian convictions.[11] One way to think of the progressive versus right-libertarian split is that progressives drilled down on a liberalism of humanitarian, cosmopolitan sentiments, while right libertarians intensified the account of competitive, economic interests.

RIGHT LIBERTARIANISM'S RIVAL BIG STORY

Right libertarians are guided by a big narrative that turns progressivism's own account of linear advancement on its head. Far from an upward ascent to freedom, these liberals believe that progressivism drags society downward towards despotism. As the title of F. A. Hayek's famous book announces, progressivism paves "the road to serfdom". It does so by allowing rights of non-interference to be violated to achieve rights of well-being. Seeking a "greater measure of welfare", progressives inadvertently set off a "necessary... chain of cause and effect" that is "bound to expand" and "become 'totalitarian' in the strict sense of the word".[12]

Better understanding right libertarianism's big story – and its predictive assertions – requires coming to terms with the central role this ideology affords to neoclassical economic theory. It is no exaggeration to say that right libertarianism thinks of itself as the guardian of a quasi-scientific theory of prosperity and efficiency. As is well known, neoclassical economics posits that individual human behaviour can be modelled in terms of strategic self-interest and a tendency to favour material over non-tangible goods.[13] The predictions of this ideology explain how agents of this kind (a species of *Homo economicus* or economic man) will act when facing various decision scenarios.

One important point to underscore is that this view of human life – as egoistic and materially acquisitive – discounts from the outset a politics of altruistic sentiments and solidarity. Rather, the optimal way to organize individuals of this sort is into competitive markets and not the incentive schemes typical of the public sector, which lead to runaway government growth. The many predictive stories told by right libertarians have this basic pattern: *Homo economicus* is most beneficially organized into laissez-faire markets, the incentive structures of the state are, by contrast, both dangerous and inefficient. A few examples of such stories will help readers grasp how this ideology works.

For example, in "The Samaritan's Dilemma", the economist James Buchanan argued that the positive rights offered by progressives predictably created a class of "parasites" taking advantage of public funds.[14] This is because no economically rational individual gives up material entitlements won at little or no personal cost, unless the calculus of incentives is changed. Indeed, if enough of a population joins the rolls of welfare recipients, they might even form a majority voting bloc lifting progressive candidates into office in exchange for reallocating wealth from the productive members of society to the unproductive free riders. In this way, a rich and free society is crushed by over-taxation and administrative bloat.

Similarly, Buchanan argued that politicians and bureaucrats, left unchecked, would pursue "self-seeking" goals and collect a "political income" while unleashing "government's voracious appetite".[15] As part of his argument, Buchanan observed that public employees faced "low price elasticity" – that is, demand for government goods remained the same even when prices rose steeply.[16] By contrast, private-sector employees contended with high price elasticity since customers with many market options could take their business elsewhere. The basic political lesson was clear: economic science predicted that government employees would be low-productivity workers, sheltered from the rigours of market competition, while private enterprises would be nimble and innovative.

Unsurprisingly, given these sorts of predictions, right libertarians like Buchanan fervently favoured policies in which the public sector was marketized to the furthest extent possible. The state might privatize by transferring administrative tasks to "private contractors" able to "supply the same quality of goods and services at substantially lower costs".[17] Similarly, austerity and budget cuts could be used to force government employees to perform the same functions more efficiently and with fewer resources.

Right libertarians also designed various auditing mechanisms to create market-like incentives for government workers. For instance, managers guided by a "decision science" could devise performance reviews and assessments (tied to promotions and pay increases) that tracked public employees and ensured they were attaining satisfactory levels of productive output. Police might be audited for the number of arrests or citations issued; teachers for student test scores. Indeed, as bureaucratic employees of the state, police could not be trusted to serve the public good and steer clear of loafing at donut shops (in one widely circulating ideological folktale). Similarly, public school teachers were likely to laze away the summers and even coast in the classroom if their incentive structures were not redesigned. One widespread policy reform was to supply students with teacher evaluations – akin to customers assessing the service or product they had just purchased or consumed. Certainly, a spirit of public-mindedness was not a reliable motivator for overriding economistic rewards and punishments. In this way, quasi-market pressures could reform the public sector. The new state need not always shrink, but might reconfigure government practices.[18]

All of this came with clear consequences for political philosophy. As Buchanan observed: from the perspective of economic science, there was no "public interest apart from . . . the separate interests of individual participants".[19] Margaret Thatcher made the same point even more bluntly: "there's no such thing as society" only "individual men and women".[20] The target of such statements was clearly the altruistic sentiments of progressives. John F. Kennedy's famous dictum – "ask not what your country can do for you, ask what you can do for your country" – was little more than sentimental, economically-illiterate claptrap. Worse than that, those who relied on such sentimentalities were flirting with inflating the state to totalitarian proportions.

A PREDICTIVE SCIENCE OF ECONOMY?

The right libertarian map thus charts both a critical project and a constructive plan. The critical project seeks to stamp out the progressive welfare state and uproot the culture of do-gooder sentimentalism that inspires it. In the United States, this effort was spearheaded by Ronald Reagan, who denounced "bleeding heart" liberals for their naïve faith in government.[21] "Misguided compassion", Reagan warned, not only sapped the American people of their rugged independence but also turned the "welfare system" into a "poverty trap – a creator and reinforcer of dependency".[22] The constructive side of this ideology, teaches that the ideal way to organize society is in terms of a minimal state, individual rights to non-interference, and competitive markets.

At this point, it is important to pose the question of how right libertarian theory justifies its key predictive claims. After all, Buchanan, Friedman, Thatcher, Reagan, and the countless rank-and-file followers of right libertarian ideology, tacitly assume elaborate forms of forecasting. Critics of neoclassical economics have long noted that its model of *Homo economicus* – on which its predictions are based – is empirically false.[23] But an approach to ideologies that sees them as cultural maps makes possible a further criticism. Namely, the insight that humans are meaning-making creatures suggests that economics and politics are both fundamentally unpredictable because they are the result of a creative, interpretive process.

Yet much of right libertarianism's magnetism radiates from its claim to rational and scientific control. As Friedman declared: "historical evidence speaks with a single voice on the relation between political freedom and a free market".[24] The scientific organization of society signals the one possible ideological option. Individuals, parties, and countries that do not follow free-market "science" depart from the canons of rationality as surely as those who reject basic logic or arithmetic. Like classical liberals and progressives before them, right libertarians, too, can come to view their own politics as mere commonsense.

By contrast, a cultural approach to ideology helps us perceive that atomistic and economistic egoism is only one possible social reality among others. Humans might instead embody meanings that contradict right libertarian rationality by telling and living stories of altruism, fellow feeling, public-mindedness, patriotism, fealty, *esprit de corps*, *noblesse oblige*, or the countless other rival ethics that can inform economics and politics. Right libertarians who deny this are attempting to harden their own cultural cartography into an inescapable geography. They are, therefore, incapable of narrating or understanding not only the rival political cultures that surround them, but also the vastly alien economies that have existed in past epochs.

This can be difficult to see because in a world largely shaped by right libertarian culture, human behaviour might come to approximate some aspects of *Homo economicus*. When this happens, the Borgesian map covers the world. Followers of right libertarian ideology then make the mistake of seeing a social reality generated by their ideology as a datum confirming its scientific universality. Ironically, right libertarianism's staying power (in spite of the fact that it cannot make good on a "science" of society) is perhaps more explicable in terms of the very cultural, ethical, and even poetic resonances repressed or occluded by its overblown claims to "science" and "reason".

Consider, in this light, the mass appeal of the novels of Ayn Rand, whose stories often present the cold mathematical and analytic themes of *Homo economicus* in a more openly narrative and poetic form. In her widely-read novel, *Atlas Shrugged*, Rand creates a hero, John Galt, who embraces a self-conscious egoism as part of a life free of social demands. Galt's oath is an alternative expression of the neoclassical economic model of humans as necessarily egoistic: "I swear – by my life and my love of it – that I will never live for the sake of another man, nor ask another man to live for mine".[25] It is also the utter opposite and complete negation of Kennedy's famous saying.

In Rand's work, we see right libertarianism's allure as a release from the burden of serving others. Followers of this map can embrace the desire for material satisfaction without bad conscience, cultivating what Rand called the "virtue of selfishness".[26] Such egoism is then narrated as ultimately more socially beneficial than altruism – market competition leading to economic growth and innovation that trickles downward. In this sense, the technical models of neoclassical theory, together with the popular novels of Rand, can both be understood as a form of ideological production. What they enact is a culture of liberalism that rejects the sentiments in favour of hardnosed interests.

Another such poetic resonance comes from right libertarianism's call for absolute autonomy and independence from government. The self-described libertarian philosopher, Robert Nozick, sometimes sounds such themes in his writings. For instance, Nozick claims that taxation is equivalent to forced labour since "seizing the results of someone's labor is equivalent to seizing hours from him and directing him to carry on various activities".[27] Taken to its logical conclusion, this argument delegitimizes any effort at raising taxes or funding government whatsoever, implying a kind of rugged, individualistic anarchy of the market.

Nozick's work helps express why political slogans like "no big government" can resonate at the street level, even as it proves true that when right libertarians govern, they do not abolish the administrative state but instead revamp it through the use of economic theory. The mobilization of right libertarianism as a historical bloc thus depends on rallying a popular base around an ethical appeal to a "minimalist state", while an elite set of technocrats governs in favour of free market logics. While neoliberalism has enjoyed popular appeal around the ideal of small government, this has proven an elusive aim when actually governing. The state has instead expanded both its managerial and security functions, as neoliberals in power find myriad administrative functions are not so easily slashed. This tension, too, is part of right libertarianism's larger story.

Over the last century many public funerals have been held to bury liberalism's supposed cadaver. Normally these ceremonies are presided over by the high priests of a rival ideology. Yet understanding that liberalism is not a quasi-organism, but instead various conflicting cultures, helps us appreciate that it might yet be renewed. Liberals of various kinds can revive its political culture by drawing on past traditional resources or introducing innovations in a way that resonates with a new generation. Such creative re-immersions in liberal politics might yet yield an unexpected leap forward into a novel form. While faith in liberalism has waned and fragmented in recent years, this is unlikely to be the last word. No one should be surprised to learn, at some future date, that liberalism has once again returned in a new guise.

4

In the name of the past: conservatism's multiple traditions

Conservatism is a cultural map foregrounding traditional society as worthy of veneration and defence against waves of avant-gardism and modernizing change. As William F. Buckley, a leading activist of this ideology, quipped: a conservative is someone who "stands athwart history, yelling Stop".[1] Recurrent themes of conservative ideology include: sacred tradition, time-tested folkways, conventional morality, inherited authority, a critique of rationalism in politics, the need for prudence, and a call for cautious and incremental change. True to its designation, the aim of conservatism is to *conserve* the cultural patrimony bequeathed to society by its ancestors. Conservatives defend the status quo insofar as it represents the visible summit of the past.

For much of the nineteenth century, American political movements did not adopt the title of "conservative". This may have been an after-effect of the Revolution of 1776, in which Patriots clashed with Loyalists who maintained fealty to the British crown. Since the Patriots founded a new regime based on ideas of Enlightenment liberalism, hybridized with various other ideologies, this likely discredited early conservatism which allied itself with the *ancien régime*. Indeed, in its original European form, conservative politics was marked by hostility to the revolutionary Enlightenment – although, as we shall see, this relationship has always been complex.

Conservatism's twentieth-century rise in the United States was pioneered by a small band of intellectuals and activists who unabashedly claimed the name as their own. These early thought-leaders sought to resist the dramatic societal changes that began with the New Deal but came to include feminism, the sexual revolution, the anti-war movement, radical ecology, the counterculture, and the rapid evolution and expansion of progressive ideology. A trailblazing work was Russell Kirk's *The Conservative Mind*, published in 1953. Among other things, Kirk conjured forth a homegrown lineage for conservatism that included figures like John Adams and Alexis de Tocqueville (neither of whom thought of their own politics in these terms).

In this way, Kirk introduced a new idea into mainstream political discourse, while positioning it as a longstanding tradition. Viewed through Kirk's eyes, conservatism was simultaneously insurgent and venerably old. This was an important feat for an ideology suspicious of novelty and deferential to the authority of an inherited past. The rise of conservatism was also buoyed by a knack for combining with other ideological maps. As we shall see, the Republican Party in the 1970s and 1980s was able to ascend by blending social conservatism with right libertarianism. So-called neoconservatives later forged similar hybridizations, envisioning liberal-capitalism as grounded in American mores and religion. But before delving into American strains of conservatism, I must clarify the sense-making features and ethical magnetism of this ideology's most consequential theorist – Edmund Burke.

EDMUND BURKE'S IDEOLOGICAL REVOLUTION

A cultural approach to ideology helps clarify that there is not one conservatism but many conservatisms – nationalist, civic, pastoral, pragmatic, religious, secular, liberal, ethnic, economic, and so on. Nonetheless, Burke's *Reflections on the Revolution in France*, published in 1790, remains a fountainhead for nearly all forms of this ideology. Indeed, this is true despite the fact that the word "conservatism" does not appear in the pages of Burke's magnum opus – although he does refer to the "conservation" of the polity.[2]

A Dublin-born, Whig member of parliament, Burke's own political convictions were famously complex. Nonetheless, his *Reflections* mounts an unambiguous and vigorous defence of landed aristocracy and hereditary monarchy – what he called the "old feudal and chivalrous spirit".[3] In doing so, Burke championed a regime that has largely vanished from the world or, at the very least, is alien to American shores. What Burke sought to *conserve* is not sociologically or historically available for restoration in the United States. If one were to enact Burke's vision of an ideal society today, it would be an idiosyncratic and anachronistic venture, like Don Quixote putting on his armour.

This creates something of a puzzle for students of ideology. If the intellectual forefather of conservatism endorsed a regime that both the Revolutions of 1776 and 1789 exiled to the past, is a Burkean conservatism even possible? After all, feudal arrangements of economy and their attendant social hierarchies have disappeared from the West. As for Burke's encomium to monarchs like Marie Antoinette – whom he exalted as a "glittering... morning star" – it might in some ways still resonate in societies with royal families, but comes off as outmoded in the democratically flattened landscape of the United States.[4]

Indeed, the vast majority of Americans can only shrug over passages where Burke ferociously denounces the "empire of light and reason" for teaching "a king is but a man; a queen is but a woman".[5] What else, after all, would a king or queen be? Some kind of celestial being? Making matters even more confusing, Burke's fervent passion for royalism in this treatise is combined with a scathing polemic against the very "rights of man" central to the American founding.

One way to resolve this tension is to draw a distinction between two different levels of argument operating simultaneously in *Reflections*. First, there is Burke's defence of a political culture already disappearing from eighteenth-century Europe. This is his ode to monarchical, landed feudalism. But at the same time, Burke is conducting a theoretical inquiry into the general ideas and principles organizing a defence of traditional society. In other words, there is a philosophical or theoretical scaffold being erected, albeit always intermixed with his defence of a particular regime.

For this reason, although *Reflections* is undoubtedly critical of Enlightenment rationalism, it nonetheless adopts the basic, modern stance of ideological mapmaking more generally. Namely, there is an effort to theorize concepts, rationally organize meanings, and mobilize political support within immanent historical time. So, while some of the substantive elements of Burke's politics remain outside contemporary life, he nonetheless offers worldmaking resources for enacting a conservative vision.

Perhaps in a former age, the premodern political traditions that concerned Burke could have been inhabited in theoretical naiveté – as if the institutions of a particular nation's politics had been supernaturally given.[6] But today, even those acting in the name of these supernatural and spiritual agencies, necessarily behave as if politics depended on human initiative (and so, in this key respect, are conservative activists and traditionalists like the radicals they oppose). A cultural approach to ideology thus makes clear that Burke's revolutionary breakthrough was to consciously theorize and mobilize tradition. This marks nothing less than the advent of modern conservative ideology. Or, put differently, the defence of tradition inaugurates conservatism as a distinctly modern map that belongs to an age of ideologies. Paradoxically, in Burke, we watch tradition become modern.

What, then, is Burke's idea of tradition? For Burke, a tradition is an inherited and unitary culture that comprises a society's way of life – from language to the arts, religion to law. It is no exaggeration to say that, for Burke, humans are traditionary creatures. This is because tradition creates the field of action and various social roles that comprise human identity. Without tradition there is no stable sense of self and neither is there a cohesive community. Likewise, without traditions there is no morality or code of ethics. Traditions are the only source individuals have for learning the nature of a good life. The more individuals move out of traditions (encouraged by the abstract and radical ideas of modernity) the more unmoored and even anarchic their lives become. Burke's heavy stress on loyalty to family, town, church and country is due to the fact that these are all part of a stream of tradition whose particularity is the only hope humans have for moral guidance, stability and growth.

One consequence of Burke's theory of tradition is that liberal individualism, with its notion that government is the result of a negotiated contract, is not only wrong but dangerous. In a well-known passage, Burke cleverly satirized liberals for believing the state was little more than "a partnership agreement in a trade of pepper and coffee ... or some other such low concern" of "temporary interest and to be dissolved by the fancy of the parties". Instead, Burke insisted politics is "a partnership in all science; a partnership in all art; a partnership in every virtue" formed between "those who are living, those who are dead, and those who are to be born".[7]

Burke's tract, therefore, offers a powerful alternative vision to that advanced by various forms of liberalism. Rather than a bargained agreement or a mechanics of utility, political society is organic, inherited, and pre-exists all members. Because humans are traditionary and born into a number of social roles that call for obligations (for example, those of son or daughter, neighbour, compatriot, and so forth), no one is, in truth, a free-floating negotiator. Instead, social roles are loaded with moral obligation and often represent non-negotiable duties. This also helps clarify conservatism's hostility to liberal globalism and multiculturalism. On the conservative view, there is no global community and to abstract away from specific traditions is to eliminate the very basis for social and moral life. Similarly, excessive amounts of multiculturalism and diversity are not good because they can undermine a society's coherence and sovereignty.

Tradition's moral authority is also linked to a critique of rationalism. For Burke, reason never unfastens or frees individuals from the traditions and customs into which they are born. Neither does reason successfully set down new foundations for moral life. To the contrary, even the greatest rationalist philosophers are unable to create moral systems with the living depth and authority of tradition. Human reasoning is weak and finite – moral authority and wisdom are either inherited or lost. Indeed, Burke's constant insistence on the need to revere inherited hierarchies is due to the fact that these are the only true storehouses of deeper human understanding.

Moral hierarchy is necessary because individuals reasoning in free-floating egalitarianism reach superficial, asinine, and even fatal conclusions. Burke, therefore, argued that the state needed to be deliberately "consecrated" and its "faults" approached "as the wounds of a father with pious awe and trembling solicitude".[8] Inside this ideological map, the traditional politics and governmental institutions of a society are experienced as sacred.

CONSERVATISM'S ALLURE

The highest figures in Burkean politics are the established authorities, moral exemplars and sages of tradition. Such leaders are steeped in the customs, mores, and inherited religion of society in such ways that qualify them to hold key offices in government. For Burke, neither faith nor morality are private issues as they are for many liberals. Rather, the character and religiosity of leaders are of central importance for judging whether they are fit to wield power.

Perhaps for this reason, those outside of conservative ideology often misunderstand Burkean theory as implying a kind of absolutism. But a true political authority, for Burke, recognizes his or her own personal limits and frailties as part of overall moral character. In fact, no individual is capable of embodying the communal wisdom of tradition which transcends all living members and even the sum total of those ancestors who came before. Wisdom has divine proportions; individuals, by contrast, are always finite and fallible. Statespersons must act with caution lest their judgements are mistaken and inadvertently destroy the very traditional lifeworld they are called upon to steward and protect.

Thus, political authority is limited for conservatives, not due to liberal principles of rights and power sharing, but because no one person can or should be trusted with a power that exceeds them infinitely. Tradition constrains and tempers every living authority's decision-making power. Political sovereignty is not absolute because it is answerable to the past. Inherited tradition and morality set down limits on present action. According to conservatives, it is precisely those who belong to a tradition who are capable of exercising virtuous limits that respect inherited customs, while both vicious people and free-floating radicals cannot be expected to perceive moral limitations on the seat of power.

One profound source of magnetism generated by the conservative ideological map is precisely this veneration for tradition and morality. Conservative reverence for the inherited past is not infrequently experienced by those drawn to this ideology as a form of religious awe. In this way, the conservative cultural map offers individuals contact and belonging with an enduring way of life that is much bigger than any one member. This traditional lifeworld then comes to be perceived as the essential, beating heart of the political community.

The ethical sources of conservatism also confer upon the traditional artifacts of society – from its food and music, to its language and mode of dress – a kind of enchanted glow. Conservatives frequently speak of traditional society as a "home" or even a "family". There is a hominess and sentiment of nostalgia that animates the conservative map. Recruits to this ideology sometimes interpret fellow travellers through metaphors of family ties (for example, a "band of brothers" or sisters; elders as "mothers" or "forefathers"). Ancestors in particular gain heights that extend far beyond mere parentage and genealogy to legendary status. No one ever reaches the same level as the founders of society once did – one lives against their backdrop as dwellers in a safe valley surrounded by snowy peaks.

As part of this, conservatism also offers a sense of injustice and even outrage: an ethical mission to fight back against the degradation of tradition by the modern world. Disenchantment and alienation are experienced by conservatives as products of secularization and radical innovation, which must be met with stiff resistance. This again implies that conservatives mobilize their ideological map from inside secular history, albeit in the hopes of rolling back or at least slowing down the pace of modern change. Needless to say, this can reach very deep into the human psyche, offering an urgent call to defend civilization from fanatics, militants, churls and philistines willing to profane all that is holy.

None of this implies that conservatives expect politics to overcome all the world's defects or injustices. To the contrary, Burke's anthropology of limits teaches conservatives to expect failure and frustration. Political gains are made over enormous time spans while their destruction can come relatively swiftly in the tumult of protests, riots, uprisings and revolutions. This points to another ethical allure of conservative ideology: a sense of sober and realistic expectations. For many recruits to conservative ideology, the appeal of the map is its matured prudence, chastened pride, and even hard-bitten realism. Irving Kristol portrayed his conversion into conservative politics as one of a former radical "mugged by reality".[9]

Conservatism therefore cultivates not only affection for what it sees as the sanctity of tradition, but also an attitude of caution or even mourning for the fragile and fleeting nature of the greatest human feats. As the conservative philosopher, Roger Scruton, put it: "conservatives often present their case in the language of mourning" starting from "the sentiment that good things are easily destroyed, but not easily created".[10] Certainly such an elegiac, lamenting tone is detectable in many enduring conservative writings – like T. S. Eliot's *The Waste Land* or Evelyn Waugh's *Brideshead Revisited*. Political melancholy, too, can generate adherence and commitment to an ideological map.

Burke once again is the *locus classicus* for the conservative idea that politics is built on arduous and ephemeral gains. This is made clear not only in his plaintive odes to medieval aristocracy, but also in his advocating gradualism lest irreverent change cause "the whole chain and continuity of the commonwealth" to come tumbling down, rendering "men ... little better than the flies of summer".[11] Conservative aversion to seismic changes – whether from the left or the right – is based on the belief that big shifts threaten to wipe out venerable accretions, leading to swarms of unintended and deleterious consequences.

THE PARADOXES OF BURKEAN TRADITION

Yet all of this also brings us to an internal dilemma for Burkean conservatism. Namely, the defence of a particular regime implies that what is morally binding is relative to place. There is no universal code or way of life. What is conservative and authoritative in one location is corrosive and innovative somewhere else. A specific branch of Anglo-Protestantism, for example, might be the traditional and conservative source of common life in one locale, but Irish Catholicism or Afghani Islam or Chinese Confucianism somewhere else. To make Burkean tradition one's universal source of political authority is, paradoxically, to relativize authority to cultural location.

Similarly, in economy one society might be feudal but another mercantilist, one agrarian but another industrial or post-industrial – the inherited order is binding but everywhere different and in conflict. Burkean theory, thus, offers resources to make whichever situation one happens to find oneself in obligatory. Conversion out of, or resistance to, the dominant culture is philosophically barred.

This also clarifies a tension between the cultural or interpretive conception of tradition, employed in our own study of ideology, and that forged by Burke. Although a cultural approach affirms Burke's insight that all politics is traditional, it is worth noting that his thinking neglects the problem that traditions themselves (whether ideological, religious, linguistic, aesthetic, and so on) are always subject to rival interpretations, developments and breaks. Traditions do not arrive as monolithic and unitary, but as fluid and contestable. Indeed, as I have been arguing all along, this multiplicity of interpretation into rival strains is evident in all the major ideologies including conservatism itself. Therefore, one problem for conservative politics is how to decide internal interpretive controversies as well as rival, exterior ones.

A cultural view of traditions cannot accept them all as equally binding, let alone sacred, because this does not wrestle sufficiently with the problem of reasoning between competing interpretive claims. Conservatives become lost in ideology when they do not recognize there is always the question of which traditions and customs within society to preserve and continue to enact. The past itself arrives in multiple, competing forms. But the Burkean map covers over this cultural reality and in doing so (super)naturalizes one ideological tradition. One map, claiming to be the official tradition of the state or the movement, carpets over all the other little fragile mosses and flowers of culture in a given domain, hiding and potentially suffocating them. Adherents of this kind of conservatism misunderstand their own identities, communities, histories and cultural ecosystems.

Similarly, while Burke rightly dissents from the classical liberal view that traditions are simply private and irrelevant to politics, he wrongly accepts the dichotomy of tradition versus rational system. For instance, in his critique of the radical liberalism of the French Revolution, Burke suggests that the latter is inherently unstable because it constitutes a highly abstract, ahistorical grid not grounded in inherited custom. Indeed, much of Burke's influential critique of the French radicals is premised on the assumption that individual-rights discourse cannot be embodied in everyday social life but instead devolves into anarchic violence and societal collapse. As Burke says, this is because the "rights of men ... admit of no temperament and no compromise" and their "abstract perfection is their practical defect".[12]

Here I must stress the ways in which various forms of Enlightenment rationalism (including natural-rights liberalism and utilitarianism) have, against the grain of their own self-conceptions, turned into inherited traditions. One of the philosophical insights provided by a cultural approach to ideology is to see the way in which all politics is forged by meanings and practices extended across generations. For this reason, one can inherit Lockean, Millean, Kantian, Jacobin, Bolshevist, or other such customs, beliefs, practices, institutions, just as one can inherit Burkean conservatism. In other words, Burke was right to see that the Enlightenment neglected tradition, but he was wrong to assume that it could not stabilize into its own set of traditions dominating a society. He took the radicals too much at their own word when they claimed to have a form of knowledge that was not traditionary. But the dichotomy between tradition and rationalistic Enlightenment – whether proposed by Burke or Thomas Paine – is false.

This is not to say that Burke's critique of rationalism in politics is wholly invalid. To the contrary, it has received a particularly impressive elaboration in the last century by the conservative philosopher Michael Oakeshott – who remains considerably more consistent with cultural insights into ideology than his more widely-known predecessor.[13] Whatever the limits of the Burkean conception of tradition, Oakeshott perceptively grasped that ideologies are not straightforwardly rational or susceptible to free-standing proof as so many Enlightenment philosophers had assumed. Rather, reason by its own lights cannot resolve interpretive controversies over the human good; this is not available by straightforward proof nor by some other method of verification outside of tradition. Oakeshott is quite right that in the domain of ideology, reason is a necessary but also a weak force.

Nonetheless, even Oakeshott's conservatism should not be understood as merely the opposite of ideology – for example, as a merely customary way of doing things, let alone a prudent pragmatism. Treating conservatism as simply pre-theoretical inheritances or practical thinking is another way to become lost in its map, naturalizing what is in fact cultural. The truth is that all conservatives must make (if only unknowingly and tacitly) the moves so typical of an ideological age: theorization, mapmaking, mobilization and world-building. But one reason this can be difficult to see is due to the deep irony that conservatism theorizes tradition.

All of a particular tradition's ideas, rituals and practices can become abstract symbols around which to mobilize a mass movement. Ideological rallying around the conservative map is in this way not dissimilar to the politics of the French Revolution. Just as individual "right" can serve as an abstraction, so too can "tradition", "custom", "religion", "sacrament", and "morality". Both rationalism and conservatism are subject to abstraction, just as they are both, in a deeper sense, textured cultural traditions. These are only apparent contradictions that are dissolved once one learns to grasp ideology culturally and historically.

Burkean conservatism thus walks a tightrope: there is an unstated hope of return or revival of a sacralized past, but also an underlying sense in which truly premodern, traditional political belonging is no longer available even on conservatism's own terms. The disenchantment of an ideological age has seeped into the conservative world picture itself. To become a Burkean conservative is already to be modern. The frequent alienation, melancholy and nostalgia of conservative politics can, therefore, in some recurrent variants have a knowing resignation to it. The traditional lifeworld of a fully sacred society has been lost to "the wasteland". And "what branches" could possibly "grow out of this stony rubbish?"[14]

AMERICAN PASTORALISTS AND COLD WAR FUSIONISTS

Whatever one makes of these criticisms, the sense-making and ethical resources of Burke's *Reflections* have undoubtedly charted a map orienting and energizing mass movements comprised of millions of individuals scattered across the West. Part of Burke's world-historical importance is due to his breakthrough in theorizing tradition as an ideological rallying point. But even his narrower allegiance to feudal and pastoral conservatism has not been entirely without influence. While throne-and-altar conservatism has little relevance on the American scene, Burke's broader pastoral sympathies do continue to reverberate with various regional and agrarian movements.

A clear case is the Lost Cause nostalgia of the American South expressed in documents like the 1930 manifesto *I'll Take My Stand*, which denounced the "American or prevailing way" of industrial capitalism in favour of a "simpler economy" of agrarian personalism.[15]

Burkean nostalgia for pre-capitalist society has obvious echoes in a desire for homespun, Southern folkways and niceties. It is also present in hugely popular Lost Cause songs like "Sweet Home Alabama", "The Night They Drove Old Dixie Down", and arguably pervades significant swaths of the country music genre. The alienation experienced by many people in the midst of liberal individualism and competitive market-society is sometimes counteracted by a yearning for smalltown life and rural idylls.

Of course, although pastoralism itself is philosophically distinct from White supremacy, in American history it has often been hybridized with it. But pastoralism in all its various fusions and iterations – racist and non-racist – and for all its diffuse reach, remains a very small movement. Instead, the dominant style of conservative politics, by an astonishing irony, has been various fusions with the very rights-based individualism that *Reflections* denounced as anarchic, unstable and anti-traditional. This is strange because it was not only Burke who saw conservatism in fundamental tension with Enlightenment ideology, but also later liberals who strenuously rejected conservatism.

In a curious historical coincidence, no less important a right libertarian than F. A. Hayek wrote a short but forceful essay entitled, "Why I am Not a Conservative". There he argued that the "decisive objection to any conservatism" was that it could not "offer an alternative to the direction in which we are moving" but is "bound by the stock ideas inherited at a given time".[16] For all its insistence on eternal verities, Hayek believed conservatism was relativistic, rendering whichever tradition one happened to be born into authoritative.

Hayek's essay is instructive because it shows that conservatism and right libertarianism are in certain key respects philosophically incompatible. This is not only due to Burke's blistering critique of market civilization in *Reflections* (which he derisively referred to as the age of "sophisters, economists, and calculators") but also because right libertarianism offers a dramatically different view of anthropology, social life, government and authority.[17] One question for students of ideology, therefore, is how the term "conservative" came to be colloquially applied in the West to two ideological traditions – right libertarianism and conservatism – whose foremost articulators appear to clash.

Again, a cultural approach helps us escape the widespread illusion that ideologies are impermeable objects with hard edges that always stay fixed. The latter is a mystification shared by countless people across the political spectrum who expect ideological labels and names to stay more or less the same across time and space. But the truth is ideologies are cultural, made of meanings, and therefore liquid, everchanging and mixable. Indeed, ideologies are so thoroughly liquid that one can even fuse their meanings when the results are philosophically, politically, ethically, aesthetically, or otherwise dubious.

Certainly, what has gone by the moniker of "conservatism" in American politics in the last 50 years is better interpreted as various Burkean and libertarian blends. This began with the attachment of the term "conservative" to a fusionist project whose most formidable advocate was William F. Buckley, the founder in 1955 of the *National Review*. No less than President Reagan later joked that he would be "lost without" Buckley's publication and that the *National Review* was to "the White House what *People* magazine" was to a "dentist's waiting room".[18] Buckley's biggest accomplishment was to envision a political alliance between the libertarianism of Wall Street elites, entrepreneurs and economists, and the traditional morality of religious conservatives.

In an early manifesto, Buckley suggested that the Cold War offered these distinct ideological groups a chance to join forces against the common enemy of "satanic . . . communism".[19] After all, the Soviet Union was at once atheist (and therefore contra traditional religion) and socialist (and therefore against capitalism). In addition, Buckley suggested that a "libertarian" state limited to protecting "citizens' lives, liberty, and property" could be combined with the "conservative" cultivation of the existent "organic moral order".[20] Buckley's tacit assumption was that evangelicals – and their allies in the conservative wings of Catholicism and Judaism – constituted a "moral majority" in the United States. Of course, huge numbers of American Catholics and Jews had supported FDR's New Deal. But Buckley, himself a Catholic, shrewdly intuited that his movement could poach these religious supporters by calling for a society in which moral discipline and self-reliance were combined with laissez-faire markets.

For Buckley, a minimalist, right libertarian state complemented a moral culture of individual thrift, temperance, chastity, moderation and industry. Those members of civil society who did not subscribe to this ethic would nonetheless be schooled into its moral code by the frugality of the state. One either learned the rigours of the ethic of work or faced the economic fallout. At the same time, Right libertarianism's muscular enforcement of property rights could be leveraged to embark on a new set of criminal justice and policing tactics that later came to be known as "law and order". As part of this, fusionism tapped into the growing alarm among social conservatives concerning crime rates, narcotics and social unrest in cities, where events like 1965's Watts riots in Los Angeles were interpreted as the fruit of progressive coddling of the poor, counterculture hedonism, and the anti-war and civil rights movements' purported lawlessness.[21]

Fusionism would not only generously fund policing at home, but also a globally preeminent military protecting the free-enterprise system abroad. Fusionist conservatives did not see a contradiction in combining small government for social services with big government for policing and military. Such an approach had complex ideological resonances across different groups and regional blocs. Some saw in law-and-order policing and Reagan's War on Drugs a straightforward effort at the moral reform of society in the wake of the 1960s. But others participated in this as part of what is commonly called the "Southern Strategy" of shifting white support out of the Democratic Party by calling for racially-coded order maintenance. This hybridization is evident in a 1957 essay by Buckley arguing that "the white community in the South" as the "advanced race" was "entitled to take such measures as are necessary to prevail, politically and culturally, in areas in which it does not predominate numerically".[22] Although Buckley later disavowed White supremacy, others retained a tacit constellation of alliances intermingling social conservatism, free markets, law and order, and racial hierarchy.

Despite its astounding political gains, the crisscrossing political allegiances forged between religious traditionalists and right libertarians remained tense. Indeed, one way to understand twenty-first-century upheavals on the American right is precisely to see that religious conservatives no longer think of capitalist markets as straightforwardly an ally to their politics. The eventual breakup would be philosophical as well as political.

NEOCONSERVATIVES AND THE DISINTEGRATION OF THE MORAL ORDER

A new wave of conservatism swapped arch-enemies: Soviet communists were replaced by liberals who embraced the counterculture and sexual revolution. The crisis of modernity was not economic but moral, brought on by individuals seeking personal emancipation and recklessly destroying the preciously accumulated wisdom of the religious past that sustained civilization. Beats, hippies, bohemians and hipsters served as an avant-garde, overturning century-long taboos on narcotics, sexual experimentation, foreign religions, and a wide-range of other customs and mores. Later, the avant-garde would become normalized, "go mainstream", adopted by the bourgeoisie and other classes as "lifestyle" choices, consumer preferences, or expressions of individual personality. Erotic licence was particularly troubling since it not only weakened the primary social unit of the family but also unleashed the unpredictably volatile and irrational forces of human sexual desire.

As part of this, neoconservatives became more critical than fusionists had been about free markets. In his 1972 essay, "Capitalism, Socialism, and Nihilism", the "godfather of neoconservatism", Irving Kristol, argued that corporations were actively disintegrating traditional morality. "Liberal capitalism", Kristol wrote, "doesn't see nihilism as an enemy, but rather as just another splendid business opportunity". Indeed, "large corporations" celebrated "pornography" and undermined "the institution of the family" more effectively than the most brazen bohemians ever managed to do.[23]

What the right libertarians and free-marketeers failed to realize, according to Kristol, was that capitalist markets were not spontaneous, natural, or universal but required certain cultural conditions. American capitalism itself was no less a tradition than Burke's aristocratic agrarianism. Kristol's innovation was to interpret liberal markets – which Burke thought of as the opposite of tradition – as an inherited culture. For Kristol this meant defending a "Puritan or Protestant ethos" of "personal merit – as represented by such bourgeois virtues as honesty, sobriety, diligence, and thrift".[24] Although Kristol was Jewish, he insisted that liberal capitalism was not a universal system but a particular set of religious and national folkways born of Calvinism and the Protestant work ethic.

Religion, on this neoconservative view, had a political role to play in promulgating the civic morality of capitalism. The credal differences between Catholics, Protestants, Jews, and others, could be bracketed in order to form a conservative bloc promoting civilizational order. Heresy from this ecumenical public religion of the right, consisted in dissenting from the moral code of capitalism. Paradoxically this brought "traditional" religionists from completely different churches closer together than they were to the progressive wings of their own congregations.

Indeed, Protestant Christians might feel closer affinities with Roman Catholics, Jews, Mormons, or even atheists and agnostics who subscribed to the civic moral code than with progressives within their own confessional communities who shared actual doctrines, sacraments, history, authority, rituals and tradition. Ideology had become more binding than theology. Or, put differently, the national *modus vivendi* had become the de facto church. The map of religion was provided by the map of ideology.

Neoconservatism had also generated a far more potent attachment to American capitalism than right libertarianism's icy, egoistic interests. Here was a politics of the sentiments but rooted in religious tradition and national belonging. Like all ideological maps, this interpretation of the world was also, at the same time, a call to change it. Moralized capitalism needed to be enacted and performed against "nihilistic" and countercultural strains of infidels (later associated with "wokeism" and "woke capital"). This would require a kind of moral crusade to keep citizens faithful to the creed – abortion, gay marriage, and many other issues would become focal points for mobilizing to retain the moral authority of the state. Conservatism hybridizes here with nationalism, discussed in Chapter 7.

The point, for now, is that the neoconservative map helped the right to interpret progressives and their allies as apostates from the national religion, responsible for heresy. A central task of the neoconservative movement was to combat these heretical beliefs and immoral practices. The failure to do so would result in civilizational decline. Indeed, meta-narratives of decline were key to neoconservative self-understanding, evident not only in Kristol's essays, but also in the far more esoteric writings of the philosopher, Leo Strauss (whose ideas concerning the decline of the West were a great inspiration to neoconservative intellectuals).[25] In this way, a tacit but familiar distinction between "civilization" and "barbarism" was revived, along with the older, republican notion that virtue sustained the defenders of the civil order.[26] After all ancient Rome had only collapsed after it had been morally sacked by the barbarians within.

Neoconservative emphasis on American politics as a civilizational project also encouraged its adherents to defend an imperial role for the United States within the international order – resisting not only the barbarism of the progressive counterculture within, but also the enemies of civilization outside the gates. After the terrorist attacks of September 11, 2001, high-ranking neoconservatives in the George W. Bush administration argued the US had a unique role in carrying out regime change in the Middle East and maintaining a global Pax Americana. At the same time, neoconservatives also hybridized these imperial commitments with the strategic preservation of parts of the New Deal, a policy agenda commonly referred to as "compassionate conservatism".[27]

At the apex of its power, the neoconservative reshaping of the ideological map deepened rifts with numerous members of the broader conservative tradition. "Paleo-conservatives" formed a nativist, ethnically homogenous backlash that insisted on isolationism in politics. Arguably the reaction against neoconservatism's globalist vision was also discernable in the complex ideological currents of the so-called new right-wing "populism" of Donald Trump – which balked at neoconservatism's stern and puritanical morality; swept aside its calls for "compassionate" policy; and ridiculed its international policies as hypocritical failures. On the other hand, Trumpism did resonate with the neoconservative effort to defend a national religion against betraying others led by permissive liberals. Much remains uncertain, but what seems clear is that the original ideological synthesis between liberal capitalism and conservatism (first attempted by fusionism and later by neoconservatism) had started to erode and reconfigure.

Thus, as with every ideological tradition under the sun, rival variations and multiplicity characterize conservative politics. Multiplicity results from followers of the conservative map facing new challenges and vying with one another over interpretive authority. Not only is society not a monolithic, sacred tradition with a single cadre of authorities (as Burke posited), conservatism itself has never achieved anything like this status.

Nonetheless, conservatism continues to resonate powerfully for millions of people. This is due to its profound cultural resources, including its sense that politics is about sacred time, that the past matters at least as much as the future, and that traditional morality is central to civic health. Even its sense of nostalgia and loss remain potently relevant. Indeed, an increasingly popular politics starts from conservative nostalgia for a disappearing past but then becomes radicalized, losing its attachments to the present and seeking no longer to conserve but overturn. This is one route by which conservatism is abandoned as an ideology – discarding gradualism and conservation of the status quo – metamorphosizing by degrees into a revolutionary radicalism of the right.

5

There is no "fascist minimum": fascist bundles and hybridizations

Fascism was born in Europe as a new kind of ultra-nationalism after the massive shock of the First World War. The historian Tony Judt wrote: "Fascists don't really have concepts. They have attitudes".[1] Although this is surely an exaggeration, it captures an important truth about fascism as a cultural map. Namely, fascists believe politics consists of ceaseless struggle, often violent, against enemies of a nation both ethnic and ideological. Politics is not primarily about justice, but a primordial clash between what the Nazi legal jurist, Carl Schmitt, called the "friend" versus the "enemy".[2]

Since politics is an existential struggle for survival, fascists are sometimes willing to strategically compromise, even contradict, key beliefs in pursuit of victory. This often leads observers to misperceive fascism as incoherent. Pronouncements like those made by Umberto Eco – that fascism is "defined as irrationalism" – are not uncommon.[3] But the truth is that fascism is far from lacking a kind of cultural coherence and sophisticated theoretical resources. However, one needs to imaginatively exit one's own map and employ a cultural approach to see how this ideology's borders, boundaries, coordinates and landmarks coalesce – something which even someone as brilliant as Eco clearly struggles to achieve.

Indeed, fascism's cartography has led intellectuals as arrestingly formidable as Carl Schmitt, Martin Heidegger, Ezra Pound, Giovanni Gentile and many others into its shadowlands. As students of ideology, we cannot preemptively dismiss fascism's ethically magnetic and sense-making features as "irrational". To the contrary, giving into this temptation severely underplays the allure of fascist politics. As with all ideologies, people become fascists because its interpretation of life resonates, and in doing so begins to saturate identity, orient action and inspire the building of worlds. Political life is not simply or even primarily about properly working out a rational syllogism or the arithmetic of some ideological calculus. Instead, ideology makes an appeal to the human need and quest for meaning. If the opponents of fascism fail to recognize this they will become vastly less effective in combatting its politics.

This chapter begins with an overview of fascist themes and motifs that emphasizes its cultural features. None of these themes is explored exhaustively and there is no reason to expect every fascist movement to exhibit any one of them. Many political scientists worry fruitlessly about defining some kind of "fascist minimum" or invariant formal aspects characteristic of all possible fascisms.[4] But a cultural approach to ideology frees us from this unachievable chore. Fascism, like all other ideologies, is a loose assemblage of meanings subject to continual mutation and hybridization. It is what the philosopher Ludwig Wittgenstein referred to as bundles of "family resemblances", in which no one trait is shared by all members of a given class across all cases.[5] Thus, as I shall suggest below, there is no fascist minimum just like there is no liberal, conservative, feminist, socialist, or any other ideological minimum. Fascism consists of assorted bundles of meaning.

I shall conclude by considering how a cultural approach both generates sharp criticisms of fascism's tendency to present itself as natural and also sheds light on the vexing problem of fascist politics in the United States – and its wider resurgence in the Western democracies. Fascism often befuddles contemporary people as it appears disguised and diluted by more familiar ideological traditions than those typical of the classical, twentieth-century fascisms of Hitler's Germany and Mussolini's Italy. But the Western democracies have for some time been busy incubating their own homegrown fascist varietals. If these are less obvious than the original fascisms, it is only because the cultural fusions in which they participate have become head-spinning in their eclecticism.

FASCI RESEMBLANCES

Fascists tell stories about a world gone catastrophically wrong. These narratives of decline often begin *in media res*: a once great people plunged into epochal crisis. The fall from grace is precipitated by some disaster – defeat in war, an economic downturn, the disappearance of traditional religion, the unseating of societal authorities, the wane of ethnic or racial dominance. Fascism teaches that these are the result of a nation deceived and sapped of vigour by its enemies. Such fatal treachery, and the attendant sense of righteous anger and grievance, is a crucial gathering point for fascist consciousness.

Twentieth-century fascism attempted to restore particular nations to bygone periods of dominance. Benito Mussolini, founder of the first fascist movement in Italy, pressed his countrymen to look on Rome as a model of past glory. His image of the *fasci* – an axe reinforced by a bundle of assorted rods – gave the ideology its name and was lifted from an ancient Roman symbol of authority. Similarly, Adolf Hitler predicted the Nazi Third Reich would rival the splendour of the First Reich of Charlemagne and the Second of Bismarck. In this way, fascist movements often tell a big story in which a betrayed nation seeks violent renewal and restoration to a past era of power and magnificence.[6]

This does not imply that fascism is reducible to political nostalgia and reactionary pessimism. To the contrary, fascists have a strong future orientation insofar as they anticipate the collective remaking of the nation. As a movement, fascism is able to bring together futurists, technologists, and those pushing a "reactionary modernism" alongside more nostalgic pastoral traditionalists and disappointed antimodernist and conservative revolutionaries.[7] There is a tense, almost paradoxical magnetism to the fascist story that combines these two opposing poles and reconciles them through the world-historical destiny of the nation that regains the past by making a big leap into the future.[8]

Although it is fiercely debated, some scholars believe that something like this ideological tension is present, albeit in hidden form, in the philosophy of Martin Heidegger – for instance in his appropriation of Friedrich Hölderlin's famous lines: "where danger is / grows the saving power also".[9] What Heidegger referred to as the "inner truth and greatness" of Nazism was its supposed unique ability to grasp the national crisis and restore the German people to their proper place.[10] The fascist tension is between the belief in a former epoch of proper order, and a revolutionary future that transcends all past regimes.

In this way, very intense human experiences of despair and hope – often associated with religion – can be captured by the fascist cultural map. Although some people flock to fascism out of mere conformism, cynicism, or fear, others undoubtedly find in it a deep sense of identity, mission, and even spiritual calling to a rebirth of self and nation. Fascist politics provides what appears to its followers as a potent antidote to a modern crisis of spiritual homelessness and nihilism.[11] Certainly fascists often evoke (again, whether legitimately or not is subject to much controversy) Friedrich Nietzsche's notion that the West faces a vacuum of meaning that must be met with a will to power that discards Judaism's and Christianity's valorization of compassion and mercy as signs of weakness and morbidity.[12]

Fascism's melding of reactionary and revolutionary impulses distinguishes it from two of its major rivals – conservatism and socialism. As we have already seen, conservatives are gradualists cautiously administering to the status quo. By contrast, fascists believe in the need to liquidate existing institutions and leadership. As part of this, fascist movements frequently exalt in the suspension of the usual moral norms, customs, decorum and traditions, in a manner not entirely different from violent radicals. Yet, unlike radicals favouring egalitarianism, fascists are utterly committed to reviving hierarchy. National rank and order is the goal, not global democratization. As Mussolini and Gentile state in a founding fascist text: "fascism trains its guns on the whole complex of democratic ideologies" and instead "asserts the . . . beneficial inequality of men".[13]

Indeed, one path by which fascists recruit conservatives is by affirming the latter's nostalgia for the past while also pushing for systemic (often violent) regime change due to the purported enormity of the present crisis. Similarly, history is filled with cases – like that of Mussolini – in which one-time socialists converted to fascism by retaining their revolutionary animus towards the existent order while dropping any faith in universalistic "humanity" or democracy. Thus, as with all ideologies, a cultural approach is sensitive to complex resonances that make an unexpected scrambling of meanings possible. Blending with rival ideologies is frequently possible – even when the ideologies in question appear to be worlds apart by the logic of the traditional left–right spectrum. Fascism is staunchly opposed to conservative gradualism and socialist egalitarianism but its big story intermixes nostalgia and revolution in such a way that it is capable of tugging on threads of meaning from both.

"SO MANY ENEMIES . . ."

Listing all of fascism's enemies is difficult because warlike opposition is directed at nearly everyone outside the movement. Combativeness is a point of pride for fascists. As the Italian fascist slogan boastfully proclaims: "so many enemies, so much honour".[14] Nonetheless, fascism's special enmity for foreigners and ethnic minorities must be underscored. Its hostility to ethnic and cultural outsiders is premised on the assumption that their presence weakens the nation and pollutes the "life space" (*Lebensraum*).

Foreigners in significant numbers present an existential risk to fascist politics – raising the spectre of racial mixing, loss of identity, depletion of finite resources and even the toppling of sovereignty. The goal is a state defined by the hegemony of a single ethnic group united by fascist ideology. Schmitt, for instance, demanded a "political unity transcending all diversity" and warned of a "disastrous pluralism tearing the German people apart into discrete classes and religious, ethnic, social and interest groups".[15] Similarly, the founder of the British Union of Fascists, Oswald Mosley, promised to put "Britain First", ridding the country of the "alien menace" usurping "the jobs of Britons".[16]

Fascist hatred of pluralism is often linked to staunch antiliberalism. Liberal ideology's encouragement of diversity is singled out by fascists as particularly nefarious to the health of the nation and worthy of eradication. Schmitt believed liberalism dissolved a people by obscuring the fundamental political standoff between friends and enemies. According to Schmitt, liberals naively assume ideological rivals can be peaceably engaged in various contractual situations like economic trade, legislative compromise, electoral politics and public debate. But, for Schmitt, this fails to recognize that politics always implies an existential struggle with the "other" and "stranger" who "negate[s] his opponent's way of life".[17]

Liberals fail to see what politics is really about and, in doing so, bring about not only the ruin of the nation but of liberalism itself. Far from identifying and waging ceaseless war on the enemies in their midst, liberals busily defend and protect their "rights". For Schmitt this means that liberals of all stripes are politically weak, believing mortal foes can be kept in check through properly designed institutions, norms and dialogue. This is why liberalism is an enfeebling and even morbid ideology. A people under the spell of liberalism "no longer possesses the energy or the will to maintain itself in the sphere of politics" and "only a weak people will disappear".[18]

By contrast, fascist movements glorify and celebrate an open militancy that confronts all ideologies, moral systems, religions and ethnic groups that would enervate the nation. Fascist rallies are regularly characterized by spectacles of strength and unapologetic cruelty either in speech or deed towards the enemies of a nation. These rallies often include public targeting of foreigners, bullying of "neutral" liberals, declaring political competitors "enemies", mocking the frail, and displaying a paramilitary aesthetic intended to render the friend–enemy binary unambiguously legible.

As part of this, brutality and fighting appear as good and even beautiful on the fascist map. Indeed, fascists frequently aestheticize violence, masculinity, military-ready bodies, weaponry, martial uniforms, camouflage, and so forth. The deeper point behind the surface aesthetic is an ideological call to mobilize individuals into the struggle to forge a nation. Fascist violence is both an instrument for restoration and an end goal insofar as it is expressive of national virility. The battlefield is the apotheosis of national striving and is cherished. "War alone keys up all human energies to their maximum tension", Mussolini and Gentile wrote, "[it] impresses the seal of nobility upon those people who have the courage to face it. All other tests are pale substitutes".[19]

Inflicting violence on the nation's enemies is a kind of personal and communal fascist ethos. At the street level, fascists often form paramilitary squadrons, gangs of muscle, male fight clubs, subversive armed cells and lone wolves. All of these can draw on disaffected veterans, police, youth groups, or male toughs. Although it can be difficult for those looking on from rival maps to appreciate, this is in fact part of fascism's fascination. Certain individuals (often young and middle-aged men) find in fascism a plan for self-enhancement, a kind of programme to sculpt themselves into one powerhouse cell within the hulking body of the nation. Individuality is achieved in opposition to the infirm bodies of other, purportedly weaker individuals and groups – ethnic, sexual, racial, or ideological outsiders. Masculinity and strength are secured through participation in the collective national body.

FASCIST ECONOMICS AND LEADERSHIP OF THE STATE

The fascist concern with collective power and autonomy is also evident in its economic vision. From the perspective of its ideological rivals, fascism is often mistaken as economically incoherent. Confusion is understandable as, historically speaking, fascists have dipped into all kinds of economic policies. These include not only social democratic initiatives to build welfare states but also doctrines of free-market organization, corporate hierarchies and protectionist policies to shield national industries and workforces from global competition, and so on.

If one believes politics is primarily about economics and not ideological meanings (as a number of forms of liberalism and socialism erroneously do) then fascist economics can be absolutely exasperating – making Eco's reduction to "irrationalism" appear more plausible. Narrow economistic thinking can also fuel baseless claims that fascism is a "left" political philosophy because it is willing to adopt some socialist ideas, albeit for narrowly nationalistic ends ("it's national *socialism*!"). But all of this misses the actual interpretive features that clearly pattern fascist economics.

Namely, fascists are intentionally flexible on economic policy, willing to adopt whatever seems necessary to lift up the ethnic group above its internal enemies and external rivals. In other words, fascists instrumentalize economic approaches – doing different things at different times by judging what they see as best for establishing national supremacy. If one is so lost inside an ideological map that all politics must conform to one "scientific" or "rational" economic framework, then fascism does indeed appear unintelligible.

Of course, the most infamous case of fascist economics was imperialistic: Hitler's *Lebensraum*, which was defended by Schmitt.[20] But the overarching goal of national sovereignty can likewise be isolationist, as in Mosley's claim that "great nations" might also be "self-contained" by taming "international finance" and protecting themselves from "the shocks and dislocations of world chaos".[21] Fascists are sceptical of liberal globalism because dependency on others is a sign of weakness. And, although fascism can articulate forceful critiques of corporations and capitalism, this typically stems from a desire to subordinate the business class to national interests, and not from egalitarian or universal humanitarian concerns with poverty (although impoverishment of the ethnic working class is an important exception).[22] Thus, imperialism, isolationism, welfare states, anti-capitalism, and free markets are all by turns bent in the direction of an ultra-nationalist will to power and the construction of hierarchy.

At the helm of these apparently contradictory impulses, steering the fascist movement, stands the exceptional leader. Fascist politics understands itself as at once a popular groundswell and a hierarchical imposition of order by one figure embodying the privileged voice of the nation. The magnetism of fascist movements often reaches a fever pitch around the charisma of this leader whose unique authority allows them to defy the norms of society, suspend morality and law, and take emergency action against enemies. Schmitt refers to the dictatorial power of the leader as akin to a walking miracle or exception in relationship to the normal governing order. Just as a miracle in nature involves a suspension of scientific law, so a miracle in the political realm is achieved by one who can violate the laws of politics and morality. As Schmitt says, the political miracle is "analogous to the miracle in theology".[23]

Although a female fascist leader is not impossible, the more common cultural pattern is, as Mosley put it, the authority of "healthy virile manhood".[24] As the personification of the nation, the male leader embodies its strength, confidence, courage, muscularity, militancy, manful fecundity and cunning. Without this dominant male figure, the nation might remain locked in a death spiral. This is the underlying reason why fascists give their leaders prerogatives and licence allowing for a range of illegalities including the purging or jailing of opponents, foreigners, protestors, and others.

Schmitt once again offers key theoretical coordinates for the fascist conception of dictatorial sovereignty. For Schmitt dictatorship is an inescapable, if repressed, feature of all politics. This is because politics continually requires someone to make decisions in special cases that suspend or exceed the law. As examples of this extralegal power, Schmitt mentions pardons and amnesties, but most important for him is when a country is plunged into a state of "exception" or emergency, which reveals the need for an "unlimited authority" able to declare a "suspension of the entire existing order".[25] The state of exception purportedly reveals a sovereign authority at work behind even the most mundane and routinized state action. At all times, "sovereign is he who decides on the exception".[26] This dictatorial power remains hidden in the shadows of liberal and rationalist legal orders, although occasionally glimpsed in open light.

Fascism's strength lies in its welcoming of the dictatorial sovereign, with unbounded power, onto the national stage. As Schmitt says, this "power is stronger... than any human good" because a dictatorial executive "himself decides" on questions of "good or evil".[27] Anything such a leader decides to do for the sake of the nationalist cause is de facto authoritative. There is no higher appeal within the movement. Hannah Arendt, who witnessed firsthand the rise of Nazism, famously observed: "The Leader has monopolized the right... of explanation" such that when it comes to defining the key beliefs of the movement on any given day, rank-and-file members must defer by saying, "'Don't ask me, ask the Leader'".[28]

Thus, societal emergency and dictatorial authority go hand in hand on the fascist ideological map. States of emergency and dictatorial takeover (as fascists take back the state on behalf of the ethnic people or nation) inaugurate an ideological worldmaking project for fascists just as surely as social contract theory and revolution perform a similar task of regime change for classical liberals. This brings us to the ways in which a cultural approach is critical of fascist concepts and themes.

DENATURALIZING FASCISM

Schmitt's idea of all states as at bottom dictatorial (even if they call themselves "democratic", "egalitarian", "liberal", or otherwise) is contradicted by a cultural analysis. The mistake is to slip into treating the state as if it were a natural or ahistorical entity whose ideological core structure is always and everywhere the same, outside the flux of culture and history. But the truth is states are inside the liquid streams of ideology and do not exist with an invariant logic or as a constant object of social physics. To be unable to see this is the effect of a Borgesian map that hides from its users the complexity of cultural reality.

Of course, fascists are often blind to this because their supposedly factual and descriptive claims about the state are, in truth, bids at remaking it. A world increasingly made in the image of fascism unsurprisingly verifies the fascistic world picture. But rather than simply discovering a dictatorial state, Schmitt and fascist politics creates it. The theory never achieves its idealized form of sovereign decider but is used to allocate increasing power and authority onto a single person heading the movement. When this happens, fascists are at sea in their own ideological oceans.

Similarly, fascists are captive to ideology when they believe themselves to be simply discovering a timeless and essential fact of all politics as reducible to the divide between friends and enemies. As this entire book shows, different ideological maps interpret the human political situation in highly variant ways. Certainly a number of the ideologies we have studied would not accept this as characteristic or central to politics. For instance, various forms of humanistic thought might claim there are overlapping goods (those of everyday social, religious, familial, or ethical life) that crosscut and are shared by people belonging to rival ideologies. For example, two family members – one fascist and the other socialist – might still share certain, immediate concrete goods of the household even as they remain opponents politically.[29] In addition, liberals and socialists each for their own part might see in all persons a humanitarian or global community.

To assume that all politics is ultimately a deadly faceoff between friends and enemies is already to have risked importing or hybridizing fascist concepts and guiding coordinates into another map. By using one's own map to colonize another, one remains adrift in ideology even as one is attempting to orient. As with the idea of dictatorial rule, fascists do not so much discover the friend–enemy dichotomy as they implore others to adopt it and use it to shape and organize their identities and societies. Emergencies and states of exception can also be culturally manufactured. In some cases, the effort to persuade an ethnic group that it is indeed living an insufferable crisis, is the first step towards carrying out a regime change and cultural revolution. The diagnosis of emergency is often a call to enact an emergency. As a form of political theatre, fascism attempts to persuade people that the moment is truly exceptional, justifying that the leader and movement take the stage and seize control. Without this securing of the proper cultural setting, one regime's fascist leader might be another regime's angry outcast.

Finally, fascism is partly characterized by an attempt to create strong adherence to party and state. But the need to continually perform an ethnic unity often results in alienating and repulsing people from the regime – not only those who refuse to perceive political reality through the friend–enemy binary, but also those either allied with or belonging to cultural groups deemed enemies of the movement. In this way, fascism's very attempt to create an idealized ethnic political unity paradoxically tears the state and society apart. The goal of total unity careens into abject weakness and disunity on fascism's own terms. Perhaps this line of thought sheds light on the ironic historical reversals of fascism: namely, an ideology that prides itself on strong and clear confrontation with enemies, instead regularly self-immolates in massive wars, often losing on the battlefield to the very liberalism it decried as too degenerate and womanish to withstand it.

Needless to say, there are many other objections that can be raised against fascism that draw on a cultural or hermeneutic approach – these include lines of critique that I shall develop in the discussion of nationalism as well as those already covered in the critique of White supremacy. Fascists often assume that humanity is carved up into natural racial species struggling with one another for dominance. But I have already shown how such quasi-biological, racial politics is bogus.

FASCISM, USA

In Shakespeare's *Hamlet* the pedantic windbag, Polonius, tries in vain to list all possible theatrical genres: "tragedy, comedy, history, pastoral, pastoral-comical, historical-pastoral, tragical-historical . . ." and so on. The attempt is humorous because exhaustively classifying art is impossible. And while foolish in the arts, this venture should be no less silly in politics. So, political scientists and historians who try to categorize all possible fascisms are not unlike modern-day Poloniuses, expecting this ideology to carry a hardened set of predictable markers. But fascism, like all ideologies, is liquid: susceptible to innumerable and unpredictable metamorphoses and fusions.

The widespread American political fiction that "It can't happen here", is strengthened by the faulty belief that fascism is either a facsimile of Hitler's Germany or Mussolini's Italy or it does not exist at all. This places indefensible conceptual strictures on fascism as an ideological tradition that are not applied to other ideologies. Imagine thinking democracy does not exist unless people are wearing togas and there is a selection by lot as in ancient Athens? Or that liberalism requires political leaders to wear white powdered wigs and activists to throw tea into Boston Harbor? Yet fascism is treated in just this clunky way – as a near historical singularity – and not a cultural tradition with continual development, growth, hybridization, innovation and variation. This is a failure of the power of interpretation.

Better to begin with a leading scholar of fascism, Robert Paxton's observation that "an authentic American fascism would have little to do with the original European models", and there would be "no swastikas" but "Stars and Stripes ... and Christian crosses".[30] In fact, "It" has already happened here as historians have identified scores of fascistic and semi-fascistic leaders and movements from the American past, including: George Lincoln Rockwell's American Nazi Party; Huey Long's politics; Father Charles Coughlin's popular radio programmes; William Lemke's presidential campaign; and Gerald Winrod's Defenders of the Christian Faith.[31] One might add to this list: the Ku Klux Klan, neo-Nazis, street gangs like skinheads, as well as more recent paramilitaries like the Patriot Front and Proud Boys. The cultural map of fascism has long had some presence in North America.

If anything, the last decade has witnessed fascism making larger advances due to successful hybridization with other more familiar ideological traditions. For example, Donald Trump's Make-America-Great-Again movement (or MAGA) has Americanized fascist themes by intermixing them with right libertarian and conservative cultures. A few words on this case might help readers develop a deeper sense for the politics of their own time as well as a sharper eye for the unexpected syntheses that are possible to detect once ideology is understood as a matrix of meanings and not a hardened, thing-like structure.

The MAGA narrative at various points echoes the fascist map, including the story of a nation (ethnically defined) catastrophically weakened and defiled by a familiar cast of foes composed of immigrants, left-wing agitators, liberal multiculturalists and conservative gradualists. Although it might mutate into something else, MAGA also presented Trump as the sole true leader of the nation who was granted privileged voice, unilateral authority, and license to violate traditional morality and norms in order to face the emergency. As Trump succinctly declared in 2016: "I alone can fix it". To Trump's bald affirmation of autocratic leadership, one might add: his encouragement of paramilitary and White nationalist organizations; inciting of the 2020 attack on the Capitol; rejection of election outcomes; threats of retaliation against political rivals and journalists; celebration of militaristic strength over weakness and dependency; and persistent repudiations of liberal rights.[32]

Yet, in spite of these resonances with fascist politics observed by many, there also continue to be clear differences with MAGA and the original, twentieth-century fascist regimes. For example, who can fail to notice that Trump spent much of his tenure as president reinforcing free-market policies and the right libertarian status quo? Where twentieth-century fascism forcefully subordinated the business elite to nationalistic demands, Trump slashed market regulations and lowered the corporate tax rate. In addition, although the 6 January 2020 attack on the Capitol was an open attempt at emergency seizure of the state, it did not succeed in inaugurating a full-blown dictatorial, ethno-nationalist state.

Dissimilarities do not stop there. Trump, unlike Mussolini and Hitler, did not primarily adopt the styles of the military. To the contrary, his cultural symbols – power suits, golf trips, gilded high-rises, country clubs, boardroom décor, slick branding – are taken from America's business class intermixed with celebrity. Indeed, Trump's entire approach to single-man rule reproduced the *modus operandi* of chief executive officers (CEOs) rather than military chieftains. In this sense, it is telling that Trump spent the ten years prior to the presidency as a host of the gameshow, *The Apprentice*, in which millions of viewers saw him in the role of capitalist boss, ejecting contestants with the catchphrase: "you're fired!".

Nonetheless, it is also evident that in right libertarian cultural personas like the celebrity and CEOs, various autocratic and dictatorial patterns have taken form. Indeed, Trump's visibility as a television boss dramatized the hierarchical structure of corporations, in which a subordinate's livelihood often hangs on the will or pleasure of a manager, boss, or CEO. Authoritarian rule is justified in these settings by familiar claims to private entitlement and market efficiency. Democracy in the workplace, by contrast, is deemed economically cumbersome and unprosperous. Might not the same be true for an entire nation? Might not the nation require the hierarchical, dictatorial structure of the corporation and its chief? In this and many other ways, corporate culture can blend with ultra-nationalist narratives to create a homegrown fascist-libertarian hybrid. (There are, indeed, more ideologies in heaven and earth than are dreamt of in our philosophies!)

A second hybridization made visible by MAGA is the injection of fascist motifs into Christianity. Perhaps the very term "Christian fascism" should be an oxymoron. But the truth remains that Christians and Christian theological concepts have figured recurrently within fascist movements. For example, although the Nazi movement had a complex and often hostile relationship to Christianity, major intellectuals within it like Schmitt tried at various points to synthesize the two. Major theologians in the German churches also subordinated the Christian faith to a more masculine and Aryan, racialized vision of Christ to make it amenable to the Nazi movement.[33] A particular tendency in the fascist takeover of traditional Christian imagery can be to render Christ more like a pagan hero – muscular, massive and omnipotent – as opposed to a violated and weak figure crucified on a cross.

Along these lines, some have argued that a new form of fascism has been launched in the United States by the evangelical "dominionist" movement, which teaches that Protestants have a divine mandate to seize control of government and enact biblically-inspired laws.[34] In terms of MAGA, the Orthodox Christian writer, Rod Dreher, suggested that Trump represents a modern version of the

New Testament "*katechon*", or a figure who "holds back the advent of the Antichrist" (the latter identified with progressives).[35] Trump as divinely appointed *katechon* is a clear rehashing of the fascist idea of the miraculous leader who alone is able to face the cataclysmic emergency and save the nation. It is worth noting that Schmitt also pursued the idea of "Christendom as a 'restraining' power" against the "Antichrist" of a fully "secularized West".[36]

Such visions of Trump as a salvific figure who suspends the law were also articulated by the Claremont Institute in the infamous "Flight 93 Election" essay published pseudonymously by Michael Anton two months before the 2016 presidential election. "2016 is the Flight 93 election", Anton wrote, "charge the cockpit or you die ... if you don't try, death is certain".[37] This was a clear attempt to rhetorically enact an emergency while appearing to simply describe it. That Trump went on to lose the 2020 election – after a paramilitarized attempt to overturn the results – and no one faced the mass death promised by Anton reveals the statement was either performative or straightforwardly false. More recently there have been attempts to interpret Trump as a "red Caesar", whose role is to lead the United States to a post-Constitutional autocratic order.[38]

In short, various complex strains of homegrown, hybridized fascism have taken root in the United States. No one can know for certain what long-term effect these novel fusionist movements will have. One could imagine the conservative and liberal cultural sources moderating or diluting fascist politics in ways that keep it from achieving the zero point of Nazism and its self-immolation in the Second World War. Alternatively, other, darker futures not yet foreseen by any living person are possible.

Regardless, many people today, reeling in the ideological pandemonium, increasingly cooperate with fascist politics not so much out of an affirmation of their doctrines as out of a rejection of the alternatives. Such citizens are propelled into fascism by a sense of moral outrage, fear and disappointment at the progressive transformation of contemporary life and the disappearance of tradition. Some might even react mostly out of narrowed attention on a single set of issues like abortion, marriage, tax rates, or "the economy". Others fearfully perceive a looming emergency bearing down upon society over which they exercise little control. They thus retreat into fascist politics the way certain crabs disappear into their holes – that is, backwards and with claws out.

This radical transformation of contemporary society, in which hybridization helps mainstream fascism, is exacerbated by the fact that even most of the leading experts are befuddled. Much confusion is caused by the doctrine of the "fascist minimum" taught by so many political scientists, historians and pundits. Such experts continue in vain to verify an invariant, generic fascism. They speak of bright lines, which like the Rubicon can be crossed and objectively determine if a given case is finally fascist or not.[39] But a more interpretive and cultural philosophy saves us from this fool's errand. We can see that there is no scientific litmus test that allows the experts to objectively verify for the rest of us whether a given person, movement, or regime is fascist "positive". Rather in politics, as in literature, no one can evade the continual need for contested interpretation.

6

Is socialism still taboo? From Marxism to Bernie Sanders

The socialist map has as its own stated goal the achievement of the most free and humane society in world history. Indeed, part of what distinguishes socialism is its unmatched sense of future potential as it self-consciously seeks to attain a form of politics that surpasses all prior regimes and epochs. Developed into a tradition during the nineteenth century, socialists expanded the emancipatory project of the Enlightenment beyond liberalism and individualistic rights. Where liberals often think of themselves as the peak of the Enlightenment, socialists instead argue that liberalism has not taken its own revolutionary promise and exercise of critical reason far enough. The Enlightenment itself needs to be further enlightened. New worlds must be created not yet charted on the liberal map.

One of the most distinctive features of socialism is its radical egalitarianism and vision of human flourishing, which it advances in the name of the entire species but especially the working class and the poor. Socialism is a form of radical humanism. Its primary nemesis in furthering its agenda is the capitalist system and its collaborators. Capitalism, on the socialist view, is not a unified society but a bundle of conflicting classes and alienated individuals manipulating one another in the pursuit of self-interest. What liberal capitalists call "freedom", socialists instead see as a self-defeating egoism that leads to cyclical outbreaks of political, economic and ecological crisis.

Unlike classical liberals, socialists do not pit individual freedom and material equality against one another. To the contrary, personal emancipation is only possible in the socialist view if substantive material equality has been communally secured. This is because most forms of socialism define freedom as a kind of flourishing that includes not only the elimination of serious material privations but also the attendant education and leisure needed to exercise higher human capacities. Among these higher-order activities is participation in a cooperative, solidaristic community that is an alternative to capitalism's status quo of individuals and families competitively fending for themselves.

Despite these and many other shared themes, socialism nonetheless experiences deep divides or rival cartographies. Revolutionary communists are often in conflict with democratic socialists; atheist materialists with religious utopians; pacifists with militants; statists with anarchists; Luddites with technocrats. Even internal to a given branch of socialism (for example, Marxism) there is heterogeneity (for example, Trotskyites, Leninists, Maoists, neo-Marxists, libertarian Marxists, and so on). If fascism is sometimes presented as anti-theoretical, no one could credibly make the same claim about socialism, which remains among the most intensely theorized of ideologies. Indeed, socialism's intellectual scope has both fueled its rapid rise and generated heated infighting. The history of socialism is marked by conflict over whether a given branch or sub-branch is truly emancipatory or instead constitutes a reactionary betrayal.

In what follows, I begin by exploring the interpretive and inspirational power of Marx and Friedrich Engels's *Communist Manifesto* as a worldmaking map. While this version of socialism often wallpapers over alternatives, it also remains the most philosophically and politically influential. As Michael Harrington – founder of the Democratic Socialists of America (DSA) – put it: any account of socialism without Marx is like an "interpretation of *Hamlet* without the prince".[1] My intentional focus on the *Manifesto* should not be mistaken for the assumption that other forms of Marxism do not exist as articulated in other texts (they do) nor that Marxism is the only kind of revolutionary socialism (it is not). Rather, my goal is to help readers appreciate how a cultural approach can orient them within socialist politics with reference to what remains this ideology's most influential document.

In the latter half of the chapter, I turn to a renascent form of socialism, which pivots away from Marxist militancy and towards various democratic and electoral strategies. The latter represents a blending of Marxist and socialist themes with progressive liberalism. Democratic socialists often hope to articulate an ideology that avoids the hierarchical and autocratic outcomes of one-party communist states that were inspired by twentieth-century Marxism.

RESIGNIFYING CAPITALISM: MARXISM'S WORLD-CHANGING MAP

Even as living memory of the Cold War dwindles, Marx's ideological presence continues to be outsized. Who, after all, has ever quite matched the scathing critique of capitalism found in the *Communist Manifesto*? Written together with Engels, it remains a paradigmatic piece of ideological cartography, a document of such colossal world-making powers that in a few pages it managed to alter the entire face of the globe.

It is sometimes asserted that Marx rejects all claims to morality or ethics in favour of hardnosed economic – even scientific – analysis. At first blush this judgement appears vindicated by passages from *The German Ideology*, in which Marx and Engels declare: "The communists do not preach morality at all . . . They do not put to people the moral demand: love one another, do not be egoists, etc", but instead "demonstrate" capitalism's "material source, with which it disappears of itself".[2]

Yet a cultural approach to ideology cannot accept this self-report as the full story. To the contrary, all ideologies have ethical sources and seek to inspire worldmaking projects. No ideology is simply analytical and free of moral exhortation, even when these features are repressed or explicitly disavowed in the name of material analysis. How the tension between Marxism's more scientistic claims and its underlying cultural and ethical sources impacts this map is a large part of my focus here. Those hoping for a survey or complete taxonomy of Marxism should look elsewhere.

Viewing the *Manifesto* as a cultural map discloses ethical depths often veiled by a mere scientistic reading. Once one learns to decode the text as a worldmaking map, it is evident how relentlessly the *Manifesto* transforms the way in which its readers experience and inhabit capitalism. From within its matrix of meaning, liberal-capitalism is resignified from an ideology of emancipation to one of bondage. As part of this, the reader is tacitly called by an unmistakably ethical voice into conversion to form a revolutionary bloc or movement to change history. This line of interpretation resonates with Marx's earlier, famous maxim: "The philosophers have only interpreted the world, in various ways; the point, however, is to change it".[3]

Consider, for example, Marx and Engels's complex effort to subvert the perception of those readers who (under the influence of a liberal map) experience contractual markets as free. Far from emancipated, the *Manifesto* suggests that wage workers in particular in this economic system are not free on liberalism's own terms – that is, able to exercise meaningful agency or choice over their life circumstances. Instead, the bulk of their time and energy is consumed by working jobs in which they have little say. The workplace for wage earners is a site not only of drudgery and mind-numbing repetition but also often endangerment and harm. Entrapment in such unfavourable material conditions is partly accomplished through systemic precarity, in which workers "live only so long as they find work" and "find work only so long as their labor increases capital".[4]

Of course, in the classical liberal map, the possibility of unemployment and loss of income is a rational part of the system insofar as it incentivizes participation in the labour market. Rather than exploitative, capitalism instead idealizes this arrangement into one of "freedom" by which is "meant . . . free trade, free selling, and buying".[5] Without the fear of the consequences of unemployment, the classical liberal story goes, no one would work.

But Marx and Engels attempt to radically reconfigure this orienting liberal story. One of many contradictions of the capitalist economy is that workers are paid least for precisely those jobs that are most undesirable and ought to require greater compensation as an incentive: "as the repulsiveness of the work increases, the wage decreases".[6] Coercion into work that is unfulfilling, unhealthy and thankless is accomplished not by economic reward but by the looming, unspoken threat of the total loss of all the goods required to eke out a living.

Neither are the hours of toil in a forced condition of labour compensated by spare or *free* time since pay is only sufficient "to prolong and reproduce a bare existence".[7] A major feature of life for the working classes is thus as a means to an end (freedom, flourishing) that never arrives because the material goods required for this have been expropriated up the class hierarchy. Fear of catastrophic deprivation provides the groundwork for mass-scale exploitation. The purportedly free contractual situation of capitalism is in real and material terms forced.

As part of this scheme, any worker unable to successfully compete on a job market – due to say, sickness, disability, addiction, a glut in labour, obsolescence of skills, or some other misfortune – lacks a livelihood and must rely on others for survival. Capitalism is, in this way, hardest on those who are poorest and most vulnerable. Flourishing and autonomy decrease as one descends from the richest (whose lives most closely approximate the sovereign individual of classical liberal ideology) to the poorest (whose rights and independence are purely formal). The exercise of liberal "freedom", in other words, is relative to one's location on a class hierarchy. Rival classes are not participating in a cooperative venture, but locked in a barely suppressed form of conflict with one another to flourish and survive.

ALIENATION AND REVOLUTION

This brings us to the Marxist theory of alienation that has been so influential in the socialist tradition more broadly. According to Marx and Engels, one important result of organizing human relations according to a brutally economistic, means-ends calculation is widespread malaise. Later Marxist theorists have drawn on this theme to argue that market civilization is historically unprecedented in the levels of mental illness experienced by its inhabitants, including depression, anxiety, suicidality, sociopathic anger, neuroses, and dysphoria.[8] The mental health crisis is depoliticized by bourgeois psychologists, doctors and health experts, but the *Manifesto* helps resignify it as symptomatic of a society in crisis.

One of Marxism's most potent sense-making features is to offer an ideological cartography for locating the endemic anxieties and discontents that wrack modern people. Suddenly this deep sense of estrangement has a political set of coordinates. It is not merely reducible to individual responsibility or biologistic explanations. Civilization's discontents are political in nature. When this reinterpretation of political reality occurs, the description is also enactive:

alienation is not simply brutely discovered in its real significance, but brought into being and intensified as carrying a certain political content. Through the very act of reading the *Manifesto*, alienation can be interpretively transformed – its first-person political and semantic significance altered. The map changes the political geography by entering into the meanings and motives of its readers.

Heightening the sense of alienation experienced by many readers of the *Manifesto* is the fact that these various forms of exploitation occur against the backdrop of capitalism's spectacular material excess. Entire passages of the *Manifesto* read like encomia to capitalism's ability to generate surplus wealth. Indeed, market civilization is lauded as the first economic system "to show what man's activity can bring about".[9] Most important to Marx and Engels's analysis is that capitalism abolishes natural scarcity.

Every economic system before capitalism was unable to produce the resources necessary for the whole human species to flourish. They were too technologically rudimentary and inefficient. By contrast, capitalism's innovations create the means to provide enough food, housing, medicine, and education for everyone. The only rub is that capitalism is incapable as a system of abolishing artificial scarcities by universally distributing these goods. A ruling class bent on preserving its power (and a way of life it deems inescapably efficient and realistic) blocks the way forward. Natural scarcity has vanished while a violently enforced artificial scarcity persists. In this way, a revolutionary urgency for true freedom can appear electrifyingly close to readers of the *Manifesto*. Is not some kind of momentous reckoning and world-changing event at hand?

This revolutionary moment – always present as an existential possibility generated by reading the *Manifesto* – brings us to a key tension in Marxist ideology. One way Marxists become lost in their own map is when they adopt a scientistic reading of their theory, assuming that what is being offered is not ethical, worldmaking exhortation but simply a description of how the mechanics of society will unfold. For example, the *Manifesto* is sometimes read as structurally predicting how revolutionary agents will arise into being. Liberal-capitalism flies apart because it radicalizes its own working class and produces "its own gravediggers".[10] On this scientistic account, the rise of a revolutionary working class whose destiny is to topple the capitalist system, is the central predictive claim of Marxist sociology. A global revolutionary consciousness is supposedly inevitable as the working class congeals into an unstoppable force.

In reality, a cultural view of ideology makes clear that there is nothing automatic or structurally fated about revolution. Any number of cultural futures is possible. Ideology can permanently forestall transition into a post-capitalist regime. Likewise, it can generate backsliding, regression, new regimes, and unexpected beginnings and endings to other political lines of development. An infinite set of possible worldmaking projects might yet be activated. Marx was certainly right to see that people dwell in epochal worlds, but wrong insofar as he assumed they follow each other predictably like a string of train cars coming down the railroad tracks of time.

Thus, scientistic readers of the *Manifesto*, who think they are merely apprehending a predictive economic or scientific document, are in fact being initiated into an interpretive grid that helps them become different selves in search of a different sort of world. This is because Marxism (like all other ideological maps) is engaged in a contest of interpretations over the very meaning of politics and human existence. Society embodies an infinitely complex tapestry of meanings, and the Marxist map makes not only a bid at offering the best account of those meanings but also a call to creatively alter them. Marx was much closer to the truth of how ideologies work when he called on philosophers to not simply interpret the world but to change it.

MARX'S ALLURE

Over the course of the last century, many people have been drawn to Marxist socialism via both the ethical and scientistic routes.[11] In terms of self-consciously ethical socialism, the *Manifesto* can activate and inspire people repulsed by the treatment of the vulnerable – the miserable, wretched and poor ones – who are exploited in the name of economic efficiency and a defective idea of freedom. Such conversions into this map are often experienced as deep moral transformations. A well-documented case is when Jack London wrote of abandoning his faith in the ideology of "individualism" after confronting "the shambles at the bottom of the Social Pit" where the "woman of the streets and the man of the gutter drew very close to me".[12]

At the same time, Marxism's sharp economistic register holds a very different set of allures for other ideological personas. Wonks, bureaucrats, analysts and number-crunchers can be recruited to Marxism's complex theory of materialism as a kind of governing philosophy or policy science. This technocratic socialism arguably reached an apotheosis in the highly bureaucratic Soviet-style states that were erected across the globe in the twentieth century from Eastern Europe to China to Cuba. Many of these more autocratic and hierarchical polities claimed to be authentic heirs of Marxist thought.

Whether or not such contentious claims are persuasive, it is certainly the case that technocratic socialism followed Joseph Stalin's exposition of Marxist ideology. In his book, *Dialectical and Historical Materialism*, Stalin claimed that Marxism was a science akin to "the laws of movement of matter" that could be used by party elites to steer societies into a communist future from the top-down.[13] Of course, from a cultural perspective the goal of the Stalinist project is unreachable. If ideologies are cultural maps, then no wonkish or technocratic class can ever fully engineer society towards revolutionary (or any other) predictable and controllable ends. Our creative, self-interpretive faculties reassert themselves.

Even leaving the crudities of Stalinism aside, the wider technocratic reading of Marxism was thwarted by capitalism's unforeseen flexibility during the twentieth century. For example, in a highly ironic set of developments, many socialist ideas (for example, the eight-hour work day) were selectively hybridized into the liberal map by progressives and social liberals hoping to humanize and stabilize capitalism through a welfare state.[14] This occurred in tandem with the baffling fragmentation of the working class into a variety of ideological maps and positions – many studied in these chapters, including conservatism, nationalism, right libertarianism and progressivism. An interpretively sensitive observer of ideology is amazed, if also unsurprised, by all these historical developments, since both the working class and capitalism denote cultural realities given to mutation and novel change, not reified or frozen objects.

Marxist communism therefore left the socialist tradition a

hugely complex inheritance. On the one hand, it gave socialism its most sophisticated interpretive grid for discerning the contradictions and instabilities of capitalist society. Held implicitly within this was an ethical appeal to broaden the reach of human flourishing to all members of society. On the other hand, it seemed to founder on the dominance of a scientistic appropriation of its politics that mistook its map for the inevitable contours of the world. Many of the twentieth-century reversals of various Marxist movements from radically egalitarian commitments to hierarchical states is due to this very technocratic and scientistic takeover.

BOURGEOISIE OR REBEL? DEMOCRATIC SOCIALISM IN AMERICA

From within the liberal imagination, Marx is perhaps the single most troubling philosopher. Where ideologies of the right – including everything from fascism to conservatism – are often treated by liberals (albeit falsely) as merely atavistic or an irrational throwback, Marxism instead poses a permanent threat. Not unlike the rivalry in religion between Christianity and Islam, Marxism is liberalism's ideological alter ego. It appears a rival claimant to rational universalism touting its own competing account of liberty, equality and enlightenment. In part as a reaction to this perceived menace, the United States has experienced various "Red Scares" which attempted to purge socialists from society's major institutions. The result was that in the twentieth century socialism appeared so marginal as to constitute what the sociologist Robert Bellah dubbed an "American taboo".[15]

Nonetheless, despite efforts at eradication, socialism has stubbornly carved out a space for itself in American life – not only its precursors in myriad religious and utopian communities (like the Shakers and Brook Farm) but especially in the mass labour movements of the modern era. Probably the most memorable early leader of socialism in the US was Eugene V. Debs whose multiple bids for the presidency garnered considerable national support. But in the new millennium, a contemporary crop of politicians – led by Bernie Sanders and Alexandria Ocasio-Cortez – has returned this ideological map to wider public awareness.

Although these more recent figures are certainly a far cry from the revolutionary socialism of classical Marxism, they still attest to the continued vitality of the socialist map by fusing its themes with liberal ideas about popular elections, pluralism and rights. As with the so-called fascist minimum, there is no empirical method of verification or incontestable answer to the question of whether Sanders or Ocasio-Cortez are "really socialist" (as if this were simply a matter of identifying a set of core features). Instead, they represent complex hybridizations of meaning that require interpretation.

Of course, no one would deny that so-called democratic socialism shares some affinities with Marxism. These mostly appear in the form of a loose assemblage of motifs and family resemblances too numerous to list exhaustively, but including: the conviction that capitalism exploits workers; the idea that liberal freedom is incomplete and defective; the political centrality of alienation and class conflict; the notion that free markets irrationally squander the common good and engender various crises; and the belief that a more democratic and humane politics is possible after capitalism has been overcome. Yet, at the same time, democratic socialists are also critical of Marxism's model for transitioning out of the seemingly infinite ideological elasticity of capitalism. Mark Fisher brilliantly summarized this predicament as "capitalist realism" in which there is a "widespread sense" that capitalism is not only the sole "viable political and economic system" but also that it is "impossible to imagine a coherent alternative".[16]

In the face of this problem, democratic socialists usually reject Marx's call for achieving socialism by waging violent class warfare. Instead, they advocate for a transition based on ethical appeals, peaceful political strategies and elections. Although democratic socialists concede that capitalist ideology has become dangerously hegemonic, they also maintain that the revolutionary overthrow of the state does little to alter the underlying social realities. In fact, doing so risks swapping capitalist ruling elites with those of the communist party. On this view, twentieth-century communism's descent from heroic egalitarianism to one-party, despotic states is symptomatic of the failure to enact a profounder conversion of the culture.

Arguably the theoretical resources of democratic socialism are older than Marxism itself, with roots in the ethical socialisms and radical republicanisms of nineteenth-century Europe.[17] Key democratic socialist thinkers like Eduard Bernstein explicitly distanced themselves from Marxism, calling for "universal franchise" as an "alternative to a violent revolution".[18] This democratizing turn was echoed by various twentieth-century American socialists. For example, Irving Howe – the cofounder of the influential left-wing magazine, *Dissent* – was highly critical of Soviet Marxism and sought a distinctly American form of radically egalitarian politics that absorbed liberal culture and rejected statist communism.[19] What was required, according to Howe, was the difficult work of transforming the culture by freely forming coalitions from the bottom-up.

Similarly, Harrington, who helped found the DSA, rebuked Marxism's revolutionary politics in favour of a hybridized liberal strategy that involved "winning political support from a majority of the people for short-run governments" that were "the only possible agency of long-run democratic change".[20] As part of this, Harrington argued that democratic socialists needed to forge alliances across different sectors of society into an increasingly diverse voting bloc. This involved a form of socialism that retained liberalism's emphasis on political compromise as well as respect for individual rights of assembly, speech, voting, and so on.

Such a socialism did not expect to establish a monolithic philosophical system akin to atheist materialist metaphysics – let alone a single governing policy science. As an alternative to wonkishness and technocracy, socialism needed to return to an openly ethical and humanistic set of commitments. This self-conscious use of ethical appeals contrasts sharply with scientistic Marxism's hostility to utopian forms of socialism as mere idealisms. But, as Harrington notes, any socialism that "is primarily economistic . . . will fail utterly" since what is required is a "shift in culture, in psychology, in the very self-conception of individuals".[21]

BEYOND SCIENTISM: THE RETURN OF UTOPIAN SOCIALISM

From a cultural perspective, democratic socialist theory marks an objective step forward in ideological map formation over technocratic and scientistic varieties of Marxism. Whatever other limits this ideology might suffer, democratic socialists who make a cultural and ethical turn avoid the error of confusing their map with an inescapable science of history and economics. They remain consistent with the insight that ideologies are cultural maps insofar as they deliberately offer a vision of a good society that competes with other visions. Harrington was very clear on this when he wrote that socialists needed to adopt a "visionary gradualism" that returned to the ancient Greek idea of politics centred on an account of "the good life".[22]

The magnetism of such an ideology is its claim to offer what both Western capitalism and Soviet Marxism were unable to achieve – namely, a truly universal politics of human flourishing. Just as individuals seek the conditions of flourishing for themselves and those they love, so democratic socialists seek this for all persons. Harrington believed this would be akin to ancient republicanism democratized, in which what Athenian citizens desired for themselves, democratic socialists demanded for all. For those recruited to this map, democratic socialist ideology offers a hopeful goal of authentic democracy as something yet to be attained. Justice still lies ahead of the human race, and not as something to merely monumentalize in history or defend at all costs in the status quo.

This is not to say there are no ways in which more ethical appeals to socialism can become lost in ideology. Indeed, not unlike liberalism, sometimes socialists can treat the supposed rational moral appeal of their politics as simply commonsense or obvious. For example, sounding much like a socialist version of Thomas Paine, the novelist George Orwell wrote in *The Road to Wigan Pier* that "Socialism is such elementary common sense" and "so blatantly obvious that ... no one could possibly fail to accept it unless he had some corrupt motive for clinging to the present system".[23]

But democratic socialists need not make such questionable appeals to the self-evidence of their politics. Instead, as part of a future-oriented politics, socialists might instead turn to utopianism as a deliberate effort at dreaming and inspiring an unexpected and even surprising moral-political transformation. This goes against Marx and Engels's *Manifesto*, which is ruthlessly critical of utopian socialism for disavowing scientific rationalism and class warfare. Of utopian experiments Marx and Engels write: "they reject all political and especially all revolutionary action; they wish to attain their ends by peaceful means ... by small experiments, necessarily doomed to failure".[24]

By contrast, many democratic socialists do not view utopian organization as unrealistic dreaming, but instead as concrete experiments with non-capitalistic forms of association in the present. The return of utopianism is not only meant to break the hegemonic hold of the capitalist cultural map, but also to form and train individuals into becoming new socialist selves that leave the old, self-interested capitalist ways behind. Utopian socialism of this kind underscores its own cultural nature and does not claim to unfold as part of the structure of history or to be available as indubitably obvious to all thinking persons. It offers a bottom-up route for overcoming capitalism.

One recent theorist of utopianism was Erik Olin Wright. According to Wright, utopian socialism consists of various experiments in intensifying and spreading democratization in the economy and politics. "Socialism", on his view, is any situation in which "the means of production are socially owned" in a "cooperative, voluntary, collective action".[25] This implies that a socialist reality already exists inside of capitalism whenever associations make a shift toward democratic self-rule. Likewise, for Wright, utopian socialism rejects "statism" or central planning (a view he associates with Marx's "state-centred socialism") precisely because it is anti-democratic.[26] Democratic socialist politics thus abandons the call in the *Manifesto* for a transition to communism by "the proletariat" seizing and "centraliz[ing] all instruments of production in the hands of the State".[27]

Clearly such a socialism moves away from an all-or-nothing regime or system change. Instead, the revolution happens whenever a new social world is enacted at the local level. Wright offers familiar examples of small-scale socialist forms of organization such as worker cooperatives in which a business or firm is democratically owned and managed by its employees. In such coops, profits are shared by all workers and management is selected to fixed terms democratically – similar to liberal notions of political representation in the state. As part of this, Wright also documents large multinational businesses run democratically such as Mondragón, a Spanish corporation with thousands of employees and billions in revenue. Market socialism is willing to experiment with different logics and arrangements without the monumental abolition of private property advocated by revolutionary communism. Again, this distinguishes it from the *Manifesto* which unambiguously calls for socialists to "do away with private property".[28]

Governmental and public sector overhauls occur along similar utopian lines. For example, Wright proposes changes like universal basic income and the spread of the participatory budget movement.[29] Socialism takes an experimental approach and is no longer tied to a monolithic agenda centrally planned by the "people's party". Socialists instead try out an array of utopian policies and practices that replace the logic of capitalist organization. Like cells renewing and replacing a body one by one, the transition to socialism happens as the constituent parts of the polity are gradually overtaken and tipped by a radically democratic political culture. If one simply lops off the head of capitalism in an act of militancy the body will remain the same.

In short, followers of a utopian socialist map work at experiments in democratizing all sectors: markets, labour, the workplace, housing, medicine, education, election funding, and so on.[30] If democratic control is at the heart of socialism, then twentieth-century statist and communist regimes were not properly socialist because they failed to be democratic. Democratic socialism therefore decentres the state and makes governmental planning a mere tool among others, not the policy essence of its politics. A cultural approach emphasizes the liquid features of socialist ideology and its ability to blend with seeming rivals like liberalism. This opens the way to a surprising range of political forms – a socialism with markets and various mixed-regime aspects.

CONTINUING CONFLICTS

Needless to say, not all socialists subscribe to the turn towards utopianism and democratic change. Dismayed by what they see as a collapse of socialism into bourgeois social democracy, some socialists have reasserted orthodox Marxism's militancy. The prolific American theorist, Fredric Jameson, has proposed the top-down imposition of a socialist state via executive control. In his 2016 essay, "An American Utopia", Jameson argued that the best hope for transitioning away from capitalism is for a future president to seize "emergency powers", conscript the entire population into the military, and universalize healthcare and education.[31] This top-down "new social structure" by fiat would then purportedly usher in "the transformation of subjectivities".[32]

Clearly this strategy attempts to gain a systemic post-capitalist regime at the expense of democracy – and is therefore in tension with democratic socialist thought. Indeed, Jameson's view of dictatorial executive and emergency powers echoes Carl Schmitt, which we already grappled with at length as a major influence on fascistic theories of sovereignty. As we have come to expect, there is nothing that bars thinkers and activists in one tradition from being highly influenced by those of another that is otherwise hostile to it. To the contrary, the permeability of all ideologies is among the central claims of this book. For example, no one familiar with twentieth-century history needs to be told that extreme, even quasi-fascistic nationalism can be combined with Stalinist conceptions of the state. It is a testament to the liquidity of ideology that such fusions are even possible.

Although Jameson surely rejects the latter, his model of regime change contradicts a culturally sensitive conception of ideology by assuming subjectivities can be transformed by the imposition of large-scale structures. Structures may be swapped out sometimes through great and violent efforts, but there is no sovereign powerful enough in politics to control human self-understanding and cultural activity. Political actors seeking to change the culture and self via executive power (a temptation for nearly all sides) are mistaken about how ideology works. Ideology is not an impersonal structure imposed from the outside, but a way of life that emerges from humanity's meaning-making, imaginative and ethical capacities.

It follows that there is no automatic structural mechanism or pathway by which imposed institutions penetrate the self-understandings and meanings of those governed. Structures do not generate "subjectivities". To the contrary, human interpretive activity is what accumulates collectively into mass-scale structures. Simply imposing a map, as Jameson proposes, does not guarantee any particular cultural outcome. The policy changes may be absorbed and received in ways that confound and scramble the intentions of its cartographers. Even the most forceful mapmakers must with awe and humility behold the way that ideology – as a collective act of meaning and significance – slips out of any single executive's or ruling cadre's control.

Meanwhile socialism as an ideological culture has been declared "dead" more times than even a historian with universal knowledge of the past could possibly tally. But one sure way to become ideologically lost is to assume there exists some kind of door that permanently closes and locks on a particular tradition. So long as we continue to live in an ideological age, the meanings of its major traditions – including those of socialism – can in principle always be revived. Whether or not they resonate in particular times and places is a sociological question and not one that can be predicted by a social "scientific" theory. Thus, there is nothing philosophically or sociologically making the dreams and ambitions of the various types of socialism impossible to reach. Socialists can continue to wager their fortunes on the claim to be the final frontier of human freedom.

PART III

Liquifying ideology: beyond left and right

7

Hiding in plain sight: nationalism and multiculturalism

We have now travelled across the ideological maps that inspired the intense polarization of politics into the opposing camps of left versus right. And yet we have also seen that this language is inadequate as we have encountered all sorts of bizarre hybrids, including revolutionary conservatives, gradualist and market socialists, libertarian fascists, communist ultra-nationalists, and more. Indeed, although we continue to use the language of "left versus right", a cultural approach reveals that there is something woefully deficient and even deceptive about this language. We should be uncomfortable with it, even if it persists as a useful shorthand.

Ideological maps exhibit subtle and complex resonances with one another, which are obscured by the left–right linear taxonomy. Indeed, it remains unclear what is being measured or spatialized across the standard spectrum, often sequenced as:

> communism (far left) ↔ socialism (left) ↔ liberalism (centre) ↔ conservatism (right) ↔ fascism (far right)

If one suggests that this ideological measuring tape is organized from the centre outward according to units of "individual freedom", or "democracy", it becomes immediately apparent that a definition from a specific ideological map is being pulled out and used to position and locate the others.

The spectrum then implies definitions of democracy and liberty that are particular to liberalism. After all, communists, socialists, conservatives, and even fascists often claim to be expressive of popular sovereignty and to achieve the proper form of liberation. Unsurprisingly, on this schema liberalism appears as not only the freest but also the most rationally "moderate" and "reasonable". As one reaches the "extreme" radicals of the left and right (communists and fascists) the tips of the line meet and bend into a horseshoe. Supposedly this is because these two ideologies are equally collectivist, statist and totalitarian. But this again reveals that this "neutral", "descriptive" chart of the world's ideologies is in fact coloured by liberal ideological presuppositions.

As if this were not bad enough, the linear language of left–right also does modern people the extreme disservice of suggesting a kind of unbridgeable gap between particular ideologies. Conservatism and socialism might appear unable to reasonably blend or mix because, after all, they are opposites on the spectrum and ought not to touch. But this is false. Ideologies are liquid meanings and can always fuse with one another. Conservatism and socialism have, in fact, cross-pollinated many times in unexpected ways. For example, one might consider some forms of Red Toryism as well as William Morris's ethical socialism (which self-consciously drew on the medievalist ideas of John Ruskin) as such hybrids.[1] There are also times when both Burke's condemnation of an age of economists and Marx's denouncement of capitalism drowning "the most heavenly ecstasies of religious fervor" in the "icy water of egoistical" calculation, find some common cause. This does not mean that socialism and conservatism are spontaneous allies. It simply means that fusions – whether politically or philosophically persuasive – are possible regardless of location on the spectrum. Thus, one will struggle mightily to interpret the political world if the picture of ideologies strung along a string like a necklace overtakes the imagination.

The final part of this book examines a cluster of ideologies – nationalism, multiculturalism, feminism and ecologism – that scholars have traditionally classified as "cross-cutting". By this they mean that these ideologies combine and amalgamate across the spectrum. But a cultural approach establishes that *all* ideologies are cross-cutting – albeit these chapters serve to further liquify ideology and abolish the simplistic picture of politics as necessarily bipolar. In fact, ideology is multipolar. Likewise, questioning the spectrum allows us to see that ideology is not like the science of biology in which certain species cannot mix and produce offspring – for example, squids and lions cannot mate to give birth to a "squid-lion". But ideologies are cultural and not natural types. Thus, the history of ideologies is filled with squid-lions and much stranger beasts, too.

I begin with nationalism, which is arguably the most ubiquitous ideology in the world. Indeed, nationalism is so omnipresent that many do not even recognize it as an ideology. It is part of nationalism to hide its cultural roots and present itself as a primordial feature of human existence. Not unlike other cartographies we have explored, nationalism often attempts to render itself geographical. When this happens, it appears that nationalist ideology is inescapable. But an interpretive approach helps show that nationalism is simply one among many possible political cultures, with its own sense-making, magnetic and world-building dimensions.

NATIONALISM AS SHAPESHIFTING

Nationalism was born in nineteenth-century Europe but quickly crisscrossed the globe. The most shapeshifting of ideologies, it is capable of becoming all things to all people – effortlessly raising its banner on opposing sides of deep political divides. Many of the big ideological fights of the last hundred years have been translated, justly or not, into nationalist terms.[2] Imperialists and anti-colonialists, capitalists and communists, progressives and traditionalists, industrialists and ecologists, theocrats and secularists, have all at one time or another avowed nationalism.

At the same time, nationalism can seep into the tiniest and most banal details of everyday life. It is capable of animating a deadly "narcissism of minor differences", as in the Balkans where it inspired "heated debates" between Croats and Serbs "over the origin of gingerbread hearts" with fights breaking out at the suggestion that one group had invented the cookie.[3] Mundane phenomena viewed as marginal or irrelevant by other ideologies – cuisine, clothing, hairstyles, sports, and music – can gain enormous significance when adopted as a marker of national identity.

Nonetheless, despite its apparent ubiquity, nationalism is a specific ideological culture with worldmaking features. One crucial nationalist theme is the primordial separateness of the world's peoples. Nationalists believe people are divided into discrete groups. What keeps this from simply being a truism, lacking in ideological punch, is that nationalists argue these divisions are both ineliminable and the fundamental basis for legitimate sovereignty – entitling them to representation in a modern state. Nations, on this view, precede states and are the only justifiable source for them. As the Prussian historian and nationalist, Heinrich von Treitschke, wrote, nations are "not brought about by the State, but existed before it".[4]

How these primordial national communities came into being can vary drastically according to particular nationalist narratives. Sometimes the story is about a prehistorical origin: a mythic clan, tribe, or race is evoked. Other times the nation is historically emergent through religion, language, tradition, or some shared experience that unites a group. For instance, Treitschke believed nations arose out of "the currents of historical life".[5] Once they exist, however, nationalist ideology maintains that these communities are independent and sovereign.

As part of this, nationalists believe we are all born into a national community. Nationalism is natural – even when it arises historically. That the word "nation" derives etymologically from Latin *nasci* (to be born) suggests that this ideology is a form of birthright politics. Part of the magnetic allure of the nationalist map is the nostalgic sentiment of having from birth been claimed by a people. In doing so, it draws on deep notions of belonging to place, culture and history. Like a second family – one that saturates and goes beyond the nuclear family – nationalism presents itself as the primal type of kinship.

Along with family, the land and environment can also become annexed into the nationalist map. Indeed, a further way nationalism attempts to naturalize its cartography is by suffusing an entire country's landscape with a national spirit. Suddenly forests and deserts, mountains and rivers, hills and valleys, all bespeak a single nation's destiny. The national territory becomes a privileged dwelling place for the community. As such, the land should not be allowed to mutually resonate as a homeland for other nations. Treitschke, for example, summons German national spirit as arising from the "oak forests of primeval Germany".[6] In the United States, canyons, highways, peaks and rivers play a similar role.

But by identifying nationalism's meaning-making features we can banish claims to naturalness and dispel the mystification of the land itself as inhabited by a pantheistic nationalist spirit. Instead, nationalism is one more contestable ideological interpretation of politics among others. Indeed, a key cultural feature of nationalism is its adoption of the Enlightenment idea of popular sovereignty. We already saw classical liberals deploy popular sovereignty by imagining freestanding individuals entering into a contract to form a government. Nationalists borrow this idea but envision the popular sovereign not as atomistic individuals but as a national will or agent. This points the way to nationalism's massive world-building project.

CARVING UP THE GLOBE

Nationalists have as their primary goal a territorialized state whose function is the representation of the national will. Treitschke asserts that "vigorous" nations "construct a State" in such a way that the "Nation and State should merge".[7] Once again, this is expressive of a typically modern vision of power, in which politics is focused on states exercising central administrative control over a domain. Laying claim to a state able to preside over the nationalist homeland or territory thus becomes this map's worldmaking mission.

As is well known, the great sociologist Max Weber defined distinctly *modern* politics as consisting of a "form of human community that (successfully) lays claim to the monopoly of legitimate physical violence within a particular territory" through an administrative and bureaucratized state.[8] Nationalists assume a modern conception of the state akin to Weber's definition. However, unlike Weber, followers of this map also tend to see the state as coalescing around a national community that secures cultural hegemony. It is the nation that holds all legitimate forms of *cultural* authority and not only physical violence. The state's legitimacy thus emerges out of the national matrix, which becomes the basic medium of politics.

But why not simply mix states with different national identities residing within smaller units such as provinces, cities, districts, or even neighbourhoods? We shall return to this question below with the multicultural rebuke of national ideology. But Treitschke forcefully articulates the tacit nationalist assumption: namely, sharing the sovereignty is either fundamentally unstable (with one group exercising tyranny over another) or else spiritually enervating as it undermines national identity and integrity. For example, writing in the nineteenth century, Treitschke did not consider the United States a nation-state at all but a "federative republic", which he suggested enfeebled its culture and made it vulnerable to fragmentation. Indeed, Treitschke believed any country not founded on a unified nationalist front would be unable to achieve "a civilization of their own in the highest human sense of the word".[9]

This brings us to another emphatically modern theme that is of great importance to the nationalist map – the romantic idea of expressive authenticity and singularity. Romanticism taught that humans needed to discover and pursue a unique way of life that resonated with their individuality. Nationalists creatively modified this idea by applying it not to single individuals, but to entire peoples who manifested a *Geist* or folk spirit. "There is no mistaking ... the German spirit", Treitschke declared.[10] Nations each laying claim to their own authentic way of life helped reinforce the need for political separatism. An authentic people required its own separate institutions and lifeworld.

In this way, nationalism often both describes and hopes to enact a world of national separatism. In fact, the descriptive and prescriptive elements of nationalism are frequently so tightly bound together that any difference is blurred. For nationalists, the world is divided into unique nations each hailing from a homeland (descriptive), therefore, politics must further demarcate and achieve this sovereignty by strengthening nationalist consciousness, overcoming rival claimants to a territory, and establishing a modern state (prescriptive). To put it somewhat paradoxically, in nationalist ideology *the map of the world must become the world of the map*.

Of course, it is trivially true that people in every epoch find themselves in a home culture. They are all born into rich linguistic and cultural traditions. But these home cultures can often have notions of politics that are multiethnic, imperial, porous, or exercise universalist conceptions of belonging. Nationalists become adrift in ideology whenever they fail to recognize that their project is a modern one of enactment and not simply a natural or primordial description. In fact, as scholars of nationalism have long recognized, this ideology must be taught and disseminated through various mass media. To achieve what Benedict Anderson famously dubbed the "imagined communities" of nationalism, entire populations must be schooled into a meta-narrative, the standardization of grammar, language, history, values, food, religion, and so on.[11] After all, nationalism seeks to rally around a state and not merely remain a collection of a few families (as in the case of primordial tribalism or clans). It is a mass politics, achieved through modern mass media and mobilization.

The state then becomes the promulgator, promoter and protector of a national culture. This means that Treitschke's doctrine that nations always precede states is a distorted simplification at best and sociologically false at worst. The truth is that states are often involved in the project of either artificially generating (even inventing) nationalist consciousness or else cultivating, spreading and maintaining the pre-existent nationalist tradition. As Charles Taylor – whose reflections on nationalism are essential to understanding it as a cultural phenomenon – observed: "It is not just that nations strive to become states; it is also that modern states, in order to survive, strive to create national allegiances".[12]

Certainly, history provides ample evidence of this strategy. For instance, Eugen Weber has demonstrated that nineteenth-century peasants in France did not think of themselves as French nationals. To the contrary, the rural regions had their own hyper-local identities and languages (*patois*) and resisted the nationalist consciousness that was mobilized and imposed by Parisians via the administrative state.[13] Far from shared throughout the territory, nationalism took hold as one provincial culture became dominant and eliminated the cultural heterogeneity of other localities. This pattern of nationalism contra locality has in turn repeated itself wherever nationalist ideology takes hold – from Italy and the United States to China and India.

One lesson of Weber's history is that far from emerging organically out of natural affection for one's birthplace, nationalism is very often coercively taught or even violently imposed. Nationalism, thus, frequently veers into the project of sponsoring a monoculture through the state that polices threats to its sovereignty that deviate from key customs and norms. A cultural approach to ideology expects this tension internal to nationalist ideology to arise, as humans continually engage in self-interpretation and creative meaning-making at the local level. Cultural mutation and change are, paradoxically, the constants of human historical experience. National ascendency and homogeneity are therefore difficult to attain for very long and impossible to achieve permanently. The nation-state must remain perpetually anxious about its cultural control. Its sovereignty is fundamentally volatile and unstable. Far from being in simple continuity with tribes and clans, nationalism seeks to achieve a cultural identity that often must correct and school local families and communities towards the national standard.

VARIETIES OF NATIONALISM: ETHNIC VERSUS CIVIC

While the defence of a sovereign, mass culture represented by a modern state is a recurrent feature of nationalism, this ideology nevertheless exists in a number of forms that differ as to how aggressively they pursue this aim. Perhaps the most important distinction, philosophically speaking, is between civic and ethnic nationalism. Where ethnic nationalism defines "the people" through exclusive identity markers (linguistic, religious, racial, or otherwise), civic nationalism instead allows for inclusion in "the people" so long as individuals pledge loyalty to a legal or political tradition. Thus, unlike ethnic nationalism, which views outsiders as rarely if ever assimilable, civic nationalism offers a path to citizenship for foreigners so long as they subscribe to the nation's legal and institutional inheritance.

Perhaps unsurprisingly, ethno-nationalism is haunted historically by the tendency to cleanse, regulate and purge the unavoidable cultural variances that arise both inside and outside an ethnic group. Ethno-nationalists are often guided by a desire for purity. After all, from within this ideological map the growth of any sizable new identity in the nation threatens sovereignty. Indeed, any ethnic group that achieves a critical mass might make a bid on secession. From the cultural perspective, there is something futile in ethno-nationalist attempts to perfectly homogenize culture and bring into being the pure sovereign. Ethno-nationalism's self-image is always slipping through its hands.

By contrast, civic nationalism is, in theory, less prone to this problem. It is, therefore, not uncommon to hear advocates of civic nationalism present their ideology as both more desirable and stable than ethnic forms. Often civic nationalists will claim that their politics only requires patriotism and not nationalistic exclusions. Nonetheless, interpretive sensitivity to ideology reveals there are important philosophical and historical differences between civic nationalism and patriotism. This point is worth delving into in detail as it casts doubt on civic nationalism's claim to offer a full-blown alternative to ethno-nationalist politics.[14]

For one thing, patriotism is a much older tradition than nationalism, going back to ancient republican thought. In patriotism, citizenship is the same as identification with the polity and only comes into full existence when some version of the political order is in place. As such, patriotism is not concerned with the unique existence of a people that precedes the political institutions.

For example, many scholars have observed that the American Revolution of 1776 was a patriotic and *not* a nationalist revolution insofar as there was no sense of a separate, pre-political people that was differentiated from the British. As the historian Gordon Wood observed, the founders "never intended to make a national revolution in any modern sense" but were "patriots" who "were not obsessed ... with the unique character of America".[15] Instead, they maintained that their basic rights as members of the British political community had been violated. This is difficult to appreciate today because during the nineteenth century the American Revolution was reinterpreted through a nationalist map. The past, today, arrives distorted and reconfigured.

In contrast to patriotism, nationalism in both its ethnic and civic forms, relies on some notion of a unique, pre-political people. Civic nationalism therefore has a tendency to promulgate, in spite of itself, certain ethnic elements. No less a civic and republican nationalist than Jean-Jacques Rousseau demonstrates this instability. Although in his *Considerations on the Government of Poland*, Rousseau penned a classic definition of civic nationalism as "love of the laws and of freedom" along with "patriotic zeal", he also made recourse to more exclusive notions of cultural belonging.[16] So, in the same text, he argued: "Always begin by giving the Poles a great opinion of themselves and their fatherland... see to it that a Pole can never become a Russian, [and] I assure you that Russia will never subjugate Poland".[17]

In this passage it is clear how quickly nationalism of all kinds can become entangled in attempting to manufacture and police a pure and monolithic culture. After all, there is nothing keeping Poles and Russians at local levels from hybridizing their cultures into something new (of finding more unity in something that is not national at all, such as their shared town or city). But Rousseau also seemed to believe that mere civic commitments were not strong enough. There needed to be some ethnic identity reinforcing the civic order and laws. As Rousseau bluntly put it: "I see only one way of giving [government] the stability it lacks: to infuse... the soul of its confederates into the entire nation" and "give their souls a national physiognomy which will set them apart from all other peoples".[18] He then went on to suggest that the national identity should penetrate into a wide range of cultural domains including literature, the arts, religion, sports, and holidays.

Rousseau is instructive for diagnosing a philosophical dilemma interior to civic nationalism. Namely, is a national civic culture possible when it includes people of radically different religious, ethical, linguistic, and other beliefs? Does not allegiance to the laws presuppose a more cohesive national culture supporting it and ensuring that a fundamental schism does not occur? Civic nationalists can, of course, move more in the direction of patriotism, renouncing primordial national identity. But this implies that the more "civic" this ideology becomes the less nationalist it is. At an extreme point, the ideology is no longer nationalist at all but a multinational and multicultural mix. Conversely, followers of this map might instead stress some notion of a shared culture or people. But this would creep towards ethno-nationalism at the expense of patriotism.

MULTICULTURAL ALTERNATIVES

Nationalist ideology may have overtaken much of the planet, but it has everywhere had to contend with the stubborn fact of not only persistent heterogeneity at the local and microlevel but also globalization at the macrolevel. In terms of the latter, the utter isolation of some premodern societies has vanished. The world's peoples ceaselessly mix and intermix in mass migrations, accelerated by unprecedented technologies, that make the planet seem small. Against globalization, many ethno-nationalist regimes work harder than ever to cleanse their territories of foreign influences and rally their citizens into monocultures. Yet the task is endless. Like snowflakes in a blizzard, people scatter and intermingle with one another.

Where ethno-nationalists call for the political exclusion of outsiders, civic nationalists instead advocate assimilation. In his journal from the 1840s, Ralph Waldo Emerson wrote that while he "hate[d] the narrowness" of ethnic nativism, he nonetheless imagined America as an "asylum of all nations" in which "Irish, Germans, Swedes, Poles, Cossacks, and all the European tribes" as well as "Africans" and "Polynesians, will construct a new race, a new religion, a new State" in a "smelting pot".[19] Many Americans still expect immigrants arriving on their shores to dissolve their cultures in Emerson's "smelting pot". On this view, deep divergences of language, custom, religion, and so on, should disappear within the first generation as a prevailing American way takes over.

In sharp contrast to both exclusion and assimilation, multicultural ideology seeks to preserve cultural difference as advantageous for political life. Multiculturalists believe that human experience is impoverished, even stunted, without ongoing exchange and social cooperation between genuinely different groups. From within this map, religious, ethnic, racial and linguistic multiplicity are perceived as assets, while homogeneity is deleterious and suffocating. One of multiculturalism's greatest ethical allures is its claim to not merely cope with diversity but to celebrate it. Multiculturalists often think of themselves as humanists capable of perceiving the good in ways of life that are totally alien to their own.

The theorization of multicultural politics is still relatively new – with origins in North America in the late twentieth century. Canada was particularly important to the history of this ideology, as it was the first to explicitly endorse a policy of multiculturalism in the 1970s and 1980s as a response to challenges posed by its own large ethnic and linguistic minorities.[20] Perhaps because of Canada's pioneering role in multicultural politics, it also nurtured some of this map's most important thinkers, including widely-read figures like Will Kymlicka and Charles Taylor.

Kymlicka rose to prominence as the chief exponent of a variant of multiculturalism that hybridizes themes of group diversity with liberal rights. Part of Kymlicka's originality lies in his forceful repudiation of a dominant liberal approach to diversity that simply tolerates differences by relegating them to the private sphere. This dominant liberal approach allows public affairs to continue apace in whatever happens to be the reigning language and culture of a particular society. Instead, Kymlicka believed this recourse to assimilation diminished both the liberty and equality of individuals in minority groups. His alternative was to expand on liberal ideology by devising a complex theory of "group" or "collective" rights for minorities inhabiting majority cultures.[21] As such, Kymlicka's multiculturalism might be thought of as an offshoot of progressive liberalism and its adoption of positive rights through an ethos of innovation and experimentation explored in Chapter 3.

A full catalogue of progressivist multicultural policies aimed at securing group rights is too vast to be attempted here, but common examples include things like: accommodations for minority religious beliefs and practices; legal guarantees to local self-government; apportionment of federal representatives; secured funding for minority schools and cultural associations; and official bilingualism or multilingualism to facilitate minority access to key institutions.[22] In this way, multicultural government seeks to create the conditions for individual equality and autonomy for citizens outside the dominant majority, who might otherwise remain at a severe disadvantage. At the same time, Kymlicka suggested that the preservation of multiple cultures across society furnished all citizens with greater autonomy by creating a substantive range of options when it came to everything from customs and language to cuisine and modes of worship. Multiculturalism was, therefore, grounded in what Kymlicka referred to as a "commitment to freedom of choice".[23]

A COMMUNAL TURN?

Not all multiculturalists believed the traditional liberal focus on individual autonomy was the best way to configure this ideology. Indeed, some instead suspected this framework concealed a bias in favour of one culture's conception of social life (perhaps, a secularized, Anglo-Protestantism with its vaunting of individual conscience over group and associational authority). As an alternative, a rival group of multiculturalists instead married this map to more communal social theories. The latter, in turn, resonated with opposing politics outside of liberalism – from socialism and civic republicanism to conservatism.

Perhaps the most formidable theorist of a more communal vision of multiculturalism is Charles Taylor. According to Taylor, multiculturalism is rooted in the need for recognition. As he put it in a seminal essay from 1992, "identity is partly shaped by recognition or its absence", and "a person or group" can "suffer real damage ... if the people or society around them mirror back" a demeaning image. For this reason, recognition was "not just a courtesy we owe people" but a "vital need".[24] Indeed, Taylor believed recognition was an especially urgent necessity for modern people who, due to their daily exposure to diverse and conflicting viewpoints, were susceptible to a "mutual fragilization of all different views".[25]

One possible reaction to "fragilization" was to mount a campaign for cultural supremacy – a recurrent pathology of nationalist politics. To stave off this semi-futile and potentially violent contest, Taylor believed multiculturalists needed to find ways to valorize entire traditions and communities. This was particularly important in cases where the demand for "self-government, as well as the ability to adopt certain kinds of legislation" were "deemed necessary for [a people's] survival".[26] In such situations, liberal rights would need to be balanced against the good of recognizing a minority group as worthy of preservation.

For Taylor, in other words, multicultural ideology was not centred on the goal of individual autonomy but on recognizing the goods internal to a communal way of life. Such social goods could not be reduced to the choices and preferences of individuals in a market. In his native Canada, Taylor backed Quebec's language laws that created an officially sanctioned Francophone space by placing linguistic requirements on individuals when running businesses, posting commercial signage, and matriculating their children in schools.[27] This policy limited individual rights with the objective of recognizing the French language as historically important to Canadians as well as securing the perpetuation of Quebecois culture. Collective political action was necessary to avoid the erosion of Quebec – through innumerable, uncoordinated individual choices – into the surrounding English-speaking majority. Taylor's own policy commitments were, in this way, blended into civic republican and social democratic themes.

By contrast, a multiculturalism of liberal autonomy risked not only breaking down the commons, but was also vulnerable to movements wishing to coopt the "politics of recognition" into commodified forms. Libertarian multiculturalism, for instance, treated diversity as a range of choices in a market. Instead of the communal self-rule of minority traditions, diversity devolved into options on a menu. In political office and the workplace (along with other socially visible sites like movies and advertisements) libertarian and neoliberal identity politics selected symbolic or token individuals for inclusion, while ignoring the plight of entire social groups and their struggle to survive. In doing so, multicultural ideology morphed into what Cornel West satirized as the politics of "black faces in high places".[28]

Libertarians and neoliberals were not the only ones able to blend multiculturalism with an already existing ideological map. For instance, conservatives could evoke the politics of recognition to bolster calls for local self-rule and the preservation of the traditional lifeworld. As part of this, pastoral conservative movements might try to shield themselves from the political pressures of urban centres and industrialization by evoking the unique value of agrarian life.[29] On the other side of the spectrum, socialists might insist that recognition instead entailed communal demands for material equality against individualist claims to property. True identity politics did not simply involve symbolic "tokenism", but raising up historically disadvantaged communities to greater equality.[30]

As should now be clear, multiculturalism is capable of liquid transformations across the ideological spectrum. No matter how these myriad disputes are resolved, this ideology cannot simply be equated with liberalism. Multicultural meanings are contested, absorbed, modified, challenged, repudiated, and accepted from every possible political angle.

MULTICULTURAL FAULT LINES

The simpleminded dualism of the current culture war falsely insists that multiculturalism is always an ideology of "the left" and of "progressives". But the truth is that like all ideologies, multiculturalism is liquid and can take on an almost maddening multiplicity of forms. In this sense, it should not be surprising to discover that feminists have ranked high among multiculturalism's most formidable critics. What to the untrained eye might appear as a case of political allies turning against one another is, in fact, a case study in the interpretive complexity of all ideological traditions.

A classic example of such feminist critique is Susan Moller Okin's blistering essay, "Is Multiculturalism Bad for Women?" Okin's central contention was that multicultural ideas, like "group rights" and "recognition", unwittingly offered cover to male-dominated hierarchies that victimized women. As Okin put it, the "politically progressive" had "been too quick to assume that feminism and multiculturalism are both good things which are easily reconciled". Instead, there existed a conflict "between feminism and a multiculturalist" commitment to "minority cultures".[31]

To bolster her argument, Okin suggested all kinds of practices that could be advanced by minority religions and cultures under the banner of multicultural exemptions and accommodations that were in tension with feminism's emancipatory goals. Although Okin did not shy away from citing extreme and fringe practices like clitoridectomies, polygamy and child marriage, she also argued that "Judaism, Christianity, and Islam" in general were "patriarchal" and exhibited a disturbing "drive to control women".[32] Feminists, therefore, needed to push back on multicultural ideology and instead opt for a progressive agenda that actively rooted out practices undermining women's agency.

The complexities of feminist ideology will need to await Chapter 8. But for now, one question is: how far would Okin's progressive feminism need to go to eliminate patriarchy inside traditional cultures? Genital mutilation might be an easy case for achieving majority backing for prohibition, but what about other practices that may be criticized on parallel grounds – say, all-male clerics and pastors or teaching children traditional gender roles? It is not difficult to imagine an entire range of practices found in most of the world's religions and cultures that would come into conflict with this ideology. And if progressivism and feminism needed to substantively reform cultures by liberalizing them, might this not be seen by multiculturalists as creating yet another imposition of monoculture? Is this variety of feminism also bad for multiculturalism?

Although I shall not attempt to untie these stubborn philosophical knots here, Okin's intervention does help flag a critical problem internal to multicultural politics. Namely, multiculturalists hope to preserve diversity; yet, at the same time, they must rely on some consensus informing acceptable or reasonable differences. For the latter to be achieved some assimilation of culture is necessary, even if it is the bare minimum of subscribing to the ethos of multiculturalism itself. Any followers of this ideological map unable to see that their politics itself constitutes a culture (perhaps viewing it as neutral or transcending all cultures) would be lost in ideology.

Taylor himself foresaw these problems as the need for some "convergence" that placed limits on what could be affirmed as part of recognition. Taylor's own solution was to attempt to imagine an overlapping consensus achieved "not through a loss or denial of traditions all around, but rather by creative re-immersions of different groups, each in their own spiritual heritage, travelling different routes to the same goal".[33] Needless to say, there is something paradoxical – albeit perhaps not insurmountable – in this ideology's attempt to hold together both convergence and difference.

On the other hand, multiculturalism in general has in its favour the ability to perceive that all politics has multicultural dimensions. Indeed, this entire book is a testament to the fact that each ideological tradition is a culture with multiple, contested and rival strains. Likewise, every ideology faces the modern predicament of the fragilization of identity. There is no split between "identity politics" and some universalist identity for politics ("classical liberal", "socialist", "progressive") as so many believe. For example, Mark Lilla is wrong when he asserts that identity politics "fetishizes our individual and group attachments" and abandons "a universal democratic 'we'".[34] Lilla's mistake is to assume that in the realm of ideology any such universal, transcendental "we" exists beyond cultural identity. While advocates of Enlightenment ideology today, like Lilla, are free to argue that their politics is universally valid, they nevertheless must begin from inside a tradition similar to universalist religions (like Islam and Christianity). Thus, joining a universalist ideology also requires cultural conversion and identity transformation.

In fact, all of modern politics emerges out of particular ideological traditions that have deep identity components and produce types of self. For better or worse, an age of ideologies is at the same time an age of multicultural and contested identities. Each map we have studied so far opens a range of identity potentials. Ideological personas inhabit the different maps, walking off the page and into the world.

8

There are many feminisms: the advent of sexual politics

Feminism began in Europe with the deceptively straightforward call to extend suffrage and the liberal "rights of man" to women. Yet it immediately became clear that this project required expansion beyond the liberal state into domains of life largely ignored as apolitical or "private" by liberal politics. Perhaps more than any other ideological map, feminism moved the politics of the "private" into the public square: from personal psychology and household labour to erotic desire and religion. So powerful has feminism's remoulding of these areas been, that no major ideological map has remained wholly untouched by it. Progressives and conservatives, socialists and nationalists, have all found it necessary to wrestle with feminist criticism, sometimes modifying their practices despite strenuous resistance.

Consider, for instance, that no mass movement in the West calls for rolling back the entirety of feminism's revolution. Every ideology now includes among its own ranks members who embrace some of feminism's innovations, such as: female access to education and the professions, the loosening of dress codes and social taboos, and so on. The boundary line on acceptable gender expressions may be vastly different according to rival ideological groups, but the line has undoubtedly moved – and the name of the mover, historically speaking, is feminism. Indeed, even the most traditional and reactionary ideological factions appear unlikely to ever fully return to the cultural norms that prevailed before feminism's arrival.

All this might lead one to hastily conclude: "we are all feminists now!" However, this would be premature. Not only do pockets of resistance to feminism persist, but males still dominate the chief institutions of power, with women also regularly experiencing inequality both in the home and the workplace. In this sense, one could just as easily declare: "there is no truly feminist society on Earth!"

The apparent paradox of feminism's universal triumph and endless postponement is resolved by recognizing that feminism is not one thing but a multiplicity of competing maps. Indeed, feminism's ideological mutations are commonly clustered into three distinct "waves". This chapter orients readers within feminist ideology by highlighting its various cultural features (such as, liquidity, ethical magnetism and worldmaking) across these "waves": first, nineteenth-century liberal rights; second, twentieth-century women's liberation; and, third, present-day gender politics.

Adopting the metaphor of three waves, however, should not bewitch us into thinking that later forms of feminism simply supplant or evaporate earlier ones. To the contrary, all three feminist waves are still rolling, foaming and mixing through time. There is no inevitable, linear development that feminist political culture must follow. Rather, its politics remain contested and fluid – pushing in dramatically opposing directions and mixing with rival ideological currents. Navigating these oceanic swells is necessary if one is ever to gain one's sea legs amid a planet encircled by waves.

BEYOND THE "RIGHTS OF MAN": FEMINISM'S FIRST WAVE

Mary Wollstonecraft's classic text, *A Vindication of the Rights of Woman*, might at first blush appear as little more than a case for the consistent application of liberal rights to women (in the tradition of the social-contract theory explored in Chapter 1). But such a reading fails to appreciate the worldmaking dimensions of Wollstonecraft's map. From the cultural perspective, Wollstonecraft's accomplishment was not limited to an abstract argument but an act of ideological creation – helping disclose and articulate a new way of being a woman.

There are strong performative dimensions to *Vindication*. To begin with, Wollstonecraft's writing is pervaded by a new kind of voice, previously deemed impermissible or even "unnatural" for women. This voice speaks not only with an absolute mastery of the conventions of style and rhetoric, but also in the rationalistic and argumentative manner of the high Enlightenment. An adroitness of writing and thought persistently and tacitly corroborates that Wollstonecraft (and with her women more generally) do not in any way "want reason". Their exclusion from the social contract is an "injustice and inconsistency" internal to liberal politics.[1]

Yet Wollstonecraft was not merely constructing syllogisms for female inclusion in the community of reason; she was also putting this community into motion. In this regard, *Vindication* became a kind of self-authenticating document and a classic of ideological worldmaking. The treatise conjured forth a female self whose authorship *ipso facto* made her a rightful member of the republic of letters. After all, writing a document like *Vindication* is precisely what opponents of female suffrage held women were by nature unable to do. Wollstonecraft's feat in turn blazed a trail for later enactive documents of the suffragette movement like Elizabeth Cady Stanton's "Declaration of Sentiments" – in which suffragettes and their allies physically (and not only metaphorically) signed onto a document of self-emancipation.[2]

The first harbingers of deeper cultural change were also present in passages where Wollstonecraft questioned the entire formation of women inside the family. In a particularly striking passage, she wrote: "Women are told from their infancy, and taught by the example of their mothers that... softness... outward obedience, and a scrupulous attention to a puerile kind of propriety, will obtain for them the protection of man; and should they be beautiful, everything else is needless".[3] As part of this, Wollstonecraft conceded the "inferiority of woman, according to the present appearance of things" but insisted that "men have increased that inferiority till women are almost sunk below the standard of rational creatures".[4]

Wollstonecraft's implication was clear: the inequality between the sexes, which seemed a plain fact of nature to so many of her contemporaries was instead of artificial manufacture. In the terms of an interpretive analysis of ideology, a map merely describing women as inferior had created a particular kind of world that in a feedback loop made this appear as part of the natural landscape. The infantilized woman, rendered inferior at the hands of her family and husband, became the indubitable grounds for her own further infantilization. She also provided the ideological foil to the woman called forth by *Vindication*. Wollstonecraft's entire authorial voice was the absolute antithesis of this frivolity and childishness.

The remedy to this situation lay in a plan of education for women that involved not only formal schooling, but the transformation of female socialization. This is one context from which to understand the nineteenth-century founding of the first institutions of higher humanistic education exclusively for women. In the United States, this cultural programme was embodied in the bricks and mortar of a remarkable constellation of women's liberal arts colleges (the so-called "Seven Sisters"): first Vassar in 1861 but quickly followed by Wellesley, Barnard, Smith, and others. Vassar's founding mission was "to accomplish for young women what college of the first class accomplish[ed] for young men", namely, the education of free and humane scholars in the ancient tradition of the liberal arts.[5]

Beginning in the upper classes, such education contributed to the radical revamping of the family, rendering it more egalitarian by abolishing the male monopoly on higher study. Wollstonecraft had complex views of marriage, but *Vindication* also foresaw a more egalitarian ideal of spousal relations at a time when inequalities of age and education between spouses were often vast. What was needed were women freed by education and character formation from "the arts of coquetry".[6] The result would be better marriages: men less bored with their wives, and women more deeply attached in equal companionship to their husbands. The latter was a cultural remaking of the family around the so-called "companionate marriage" – or a bond between spouses, relatively equal in development.

Arguably this vision of family life received articulation in the brilliant novels of Jane Austen. *Pride and Prejudice*, for instance, presented a range of female and male characters in and around the Bennet family, some in favour of greater egalitarianism and classical virtue for women (for example, Elizabeth, Jane, Mr Bennet and Mr Darcy) and others against it (for example, Lydia, Kitty, Mrs Bennet and Mr Wickham). Much of the drama of the narrative swirls around whether the achievement of a true marriage of minds and virtue will become possible (the new companionate mode), or, if instead, the women will be infantilized amid the shallow, vicious, vain, flirtatious and duplicitous schemes of those who still hold to the older mode.

One reason for the astonishing spread of the first wave of feminism was that it proposed a culture of self and family that increasing numbers of people found ethically attractive. Indeed, the vision of a more egalitarian marriage, tacitly evident in Austen's novels, continues to resonate powerfully with millions of individuals across the ideological spectrum who hybridize it with heterogenous traditions. Thus, first-wave feminism has seeped into the social world at a ground level, often changing the lives of those who subscribe to ideologies that officially, staunchly oppose feminism.[7]

First-wave feminism's magnetism is, therefore, partly attributable to its claim to make possible a more hopeful, even jubilant set of relationships. This is often lost sight of as the focus tends to be on feminism's harder or critical side, which is sometimes caricatured into the ideological spectre of the unhappy, discontented feminist.[8] But far from simply extending a formal grid of rights to already autonomous women, first-wave feminism created a new culture in which it would become eminently reasonable, even a joyful event (like one of Austen's idealized marriages), for the greater equality of women to be accomplished.

AGAINST PATRIARCHY: FEMINISM'S SECOND WAVE

Early stirrings of a second wave are sometimes attributed to the French existentialist philosopher, Simone de Beauvoir, and her tremendously influential aphorism from *The Second Sex*: "One is not born, but rather becomes, woman".[9] Whether this is anachronistic or not, it is nonetheless safe to say Beauvoir's thinking served as a key reference point for second-wave feminism's more intense turn towards existential questions. What was in play was no longer just the social contract, education and character formation, but the entire existential status and significance of being and becoming a woman.

In the United States, a postwar existential malaise received articulation in Betty Friedan's *The Feminine Mystique*. Published in 1963, Friedan's book popularized the image of the housewife afflicted by the "same deadly 'dailyness'" and "the terror of the problem that has no name".[10] One important feature of the problem with "no name" was the socio-psychological sense of being trapped – of depression, anxiety, anger and frustration at being blocked from advancement outside the household.

But an obscurer problem was also present, as evident in Sylvia Plath's famous poem, "Daddy", written one year before *The Feminine Mystique*. Plath (who like Friedan had been educated at one of the Seven Sisters colleges) drafted a profoundly cryptic poem, in which she pictured the father–daughter relationship as one between a German fascist and a Jew. Although the poem ultimately recounted a patricide – in which the daughter (metaphorically?) killed her father – this was not accomplished before she confessed: "Every woman adores a Fascist / The boot in the face".[11]

Second-wave feminism would insist that the puzzle of female entanglement in male domination was much trickier than any first-wave theorist had imagined. Modern psychoanalysis and depth psychology had discovered a shadowy terra incognita – a land of traumas and repressions – that existed as much inside a woman as outside of her. An all-invasive form of male domination that it gave the name of "patriarchy" began to come into view. Against patriarchy, a cultural revolution would be required that liberated the female subject from the ground up and inside out.

Nineteen-sixties "women's liberation" coalesced as a mass movement around the goal of toppling authoritarian male domination in all its guises. A key theorization of this map was offered by Kate Millett and her 1968 treatise, *Sexual Politics*. There Millett defined "patriarchy" as rule by biological males, symbolically figured in the father, and suggested that this type of power pervaded every major social institution as well as the internal psyches of women.[12]

According to Millett, patriarchy was "the most pervasive ideology of our culture", present in "every avenue of power" including "the military, industry, technology, universities, science, political office, and finance". Even "supernatural authority, the Deity, 'His' ministry" was of "male manufacture".[13] Indeed, for second-wave feminists, patriarchy was so englobing, so naturalizing, that it promulgated not only its own anthropology but an entire metaphysics. Patriarchal societies gazed out into the cosmos and saw in the mirror of the stars, their own system of power. In the West this was evident in Hebraic and Christian monotheism as well as Greek mythology.

The destruction of patriarchy implied a politics that grew increasingly incompatible with liberalism's depoliticization of the private. A popular slogan of women's liberation became: "the personal is political". This was a result of having further complicated the oppressor–oppressed dichotomy. Millett argued women had been subject to an intrusive "interior colonization", in which the adoption of patriarchal ideology took hold of their very self-understandings.[14] Patriarchal societies did not simply consist of biological men outwardly exercising control over biological women. Rather, women had been indoctrinated into complicity with patriarchy inside the deepest recesses of their identity.

Hybridization of second-wave feminism with the practices of clinical psychology, therapy and healing, thus became an important part of this ideology. Women's liberation had as an aim not only the feminist reform of medicine and psychology, but also the absorption of many of its methods and theories as key instruments in the difficult interior work of purging patriarchy and overcoming traumas. One ethically magnetic feature of this map was to offer an interpretive matrix for confronting one's own biographical wounds and injuries growing up in patriarchal families. Through depth psychology, feminists began to confront the angry, bullying "daddy" of Plath's poem, as well as the subtly nice father who nonetheless tacitly assumed the privileges and hierarchies of a patriarchal system.

Women's liberation also raised consciousness of sexuality as a site for patriarchy's control and punishment of female bodies. For example, in erotic relations patriarchal societies emphasized that the woman was an object and the man a subject who performed different verbs. As the feminist legal scholar, Catharine MacKinnon, jarringly put it: "Sexual objectification is the primary process of the subjection of women ... Man fucks woman; subject verb object".[15] This passivity had already been discussed by Millett in terms of a pattern of erotic relations in patriarchal cultures where women internalized masochism and men sadism.[16] Mobilization around reproductive and contraceptive practices was seen by followers of this cartography as an essential method of resistance to the reduction of female bodies to the functions of sexual intercourse, reproduction and maternity.

Yet herein also lies much of the polarization and controversy around the second wave. So total was the critique of traditional cultures as patriarchal, that to some the requirements for feminist liberation began to appear unacceptably high – implying the abandonment, even abolition of many of the world's traditional cultures. Did second-wave feminism necessitate the achievement of a single, post-patriarchal monoculture? If so, it would fall into many of the interpretive dilemmas of all ideological maps that require such a high level of ethical and political uniformity. Or might the dismantling of patriarchy instead find a way of affirming and valorizing the customs, religions and cultures that preceded it?

SEX VERSUS GENDER TROUBLE

Among the most momentous ideological innovations introduced by second-wave feminism was the sex versus gender distinction. Sex, on this view, was the biological classification of males and females according to various reproductive traits. Gender, by contrast, consisted of cultural roles and norms of conduct said to properly and ideally represent a person's underlying sex.

Millett argued that in patriarchal cultures the feminine gender was forcefully imposed onto biological women. Beginning at birth, the female sex was severely disciplined into conforming to behaviours said to be conducive to reproduction and motherhood, including emotionality, passivity, tenderness, receptivity. As part of this, the female sex was also barred from behaviours said to be masculine and thereby reserved for the male sex. These included aspects of personality (like competitiveness, forcefulness, creativity and braininess) as well as access to certain social domains (such as, politics, sports, business, the arts, and sciences). In this way, "domestic service and attendance upon infants" was assigned "to the female" and "the rest of human achievement, interest, and ambition to the male".[17]

Adolescence was especially fraught because it was the period of development in which patriarchy insisted that conformity to gender was absolutely mandatory. Girls, who might have spent their childhoods as more analytical, aggressive, rough and tumble, or funny than the boys, were suddenly subject to a "merciless task of conformity" to "gender identity", causing a strain that could reach "crisis proportions" and even mental breakdown.[18] Boys also suffered psychic damage from coercive corrections towards masculinity, albeit these were significantly offset by the retention of greater privileges and power.

The establishment of sex versus gender as an ideological distinction also helped locate one of second-wave feminism's central emancipatory goals: the subversion of patriarchy's system of gender. Women's liberation would deconstruct the feminine gender both by violating norms of conduct and showing that women could excel in roles previously deemed masculine. In this way, what patriarchy presented as falsely natural (the unchangeable fate of the female sex) would be revealed as cultural and contingent. Or, to put it in the terms of our own interpretive analysis of ideology: patriarchy's naturalization of gender was a case of a Borgesian map usurping the world.

Yet, for all their criticisms of "sex", second-wave feminists also retained the concept as essential for demarcating the ideology of the women's movement itself. Millett's entire analysis assumed an essential biological dichotomy, what she called the "situation between the sexes ... throughout history" in which "that half of the populace which is female is controlled by that half which is male".[19] In a strange irony of history, second-wave feminism in its effort to denaturalize patriarchy had ended up naturalizing the politics of the women's movement as centred on a pre-cultural female subject. By this route, we arrive at one of the largest schisms to date in feminist ideology: namely, some feminists would remain within Millett's notion that feminism was primarily about emancipating biological women, while others did not.

Chief among the latter was Judith Butler, who opened her authoritative 1990 text, *Gender Trouble*, with a blunt criticism of earlier feminism for assuming "there is some existing identity, understood through the category of women" with unified "interests and goals" as a universal "subject of feminism".[20] In truth, Butler argued, the latter was a "fictive ... foundationalist fable" that attempted to "emancipate an essence ... which cannot be found".[21] From a cultural perspective of ideology, second-wave feminists were right to denaturalize patriarchy, but Butler was correct to denaturalize women's liberation. Both movements needed to be understood as ideological traditions and not as a politics of brutely given nature.

At the same time, Butler pushed feminism into newer and more difficult philosophical territory with her claim that "sex" itself was an effect of gender. "Perhaps this construct called 'sex,'" she wrote, "is as culturally constructed as gender" such that "the distinction between sex and gender turns out to be no distinction at all".[22] The debate over to what extent biological sex is collapsible into gender has raged ever since – not merely in philosophy journals but increasingly in everyday life.[23] As the feminist philosopher, Georgia Warnke, put this puzzle: "Does sex cause gender . . . ? [Or] conversely does gender so thoroughly cause sex that sex is in fact nothing but gender?"[24]

To make matters even more confusing, some feminists responded by reasserting the categories of both sex and gender – a phenomenon sometimes referred to as deradicalization. For example, Camille Paglia received a considerable amount of attention in the 1990s for asserting that feminism had fallen into a "constructionist bias" that "never thinks about nature" and therefore "cannot deal with sex".[25] According to Paglia, sex not only remained a distinct and natural category but at least some aspects of the traditional masculine and feminine genders correlated with it.[26]

Although it is not my task to take a position in these ongoing debates, which are internal to feminism itself, it is important to see that this ideology has dispersed into a bewildering range of possible rival forms. One common way to demarcate third-wave feminism from prior maps is precisely to observe its heightened sense of multiplicity and contestation. Certainly no one could plausibly claim that third-wave "feminism" represented a single, monolithic political bloc.

GENDER AND IDEOLOGICAL FLUIDITY: FEMINISM'S THIRD WAVE

Feminism's third wave gained momentum by widening its ideological map to include a sexual politics of gender encompassing not only women but gay, lesbian, transgender, and other nonconforming people as key to mobilization. Simultaneously, intersectionality theorists criticized the second wave for assuming there was a universal experience of womanhood apart from the realities of race and class. Bell hooks, for example, wrote influential pieces arguing that under a falsely universal banner of the female sex, women's liberation had "suppressed and denied" the role of "whiteness" as a "privileged category" offering a falsely colourblind "vision of sisterhood" and "eliminating race from the picture".[27]

The most philosophically wide-ranging basis for a feminist map based on the multiplicity of genders (and not the female sex) was offered by Butler. Specifically, Butler introduced the concept of gender performativity. "Gender", she wrote, "is in no way a stable identity or locus of agency... rather, it is... an identity instituted through a *stylized repetition of acts*" that create the "illusion of an abiding gendered self".[28] Gender was policed and controlled by society (as second-wave feminists had already seen), but it was in no way a system limited to the female sex. To the contrary, sex itself was a category of knowledge produced by the politics of gender. Butler thus made possible a feminism that turned away from the defence of biological females to a politics of gender fluidity.

Crucial to Butler's theory was that one could *not* simply select a gender like clothes from "the closet", wear it "for the day" and restore "the garment to its place at night".[29] Rather, gender was an entire set of practices that while subject to individual resistance, was also disciplined into the entire social body. One did not simply "do gender" so to speak, but gender always preceded individuals through their cultural and political context (gender was also "done" to you).

For example, Butler discussed not only pressure to conform sexual desire to heterosexual patterns but also cultural practices like the "patronymic" by which "wives and daughters, relinquish their name and secure perpetuity and rigidity for some other patronym".[30] In such a naming culture, gender always preceded the participants. Going against the grain to recover a matronymic name might not always be possible as it was lost to history (or at least came with informal and formal social costs). In this way, gender was inherited as a system even if it could be creatively bent, scrambled, or modified in ways that subverted the dominant culture of conformity.

This is how to understand Butler's claims that "drag, cross-dressing... butch/femme identities" and other forms of gender non-conformity subverted "the notion of a true gender identity" anchored in the heterosexual norms organizing clothing, gestures, expressions, manners and desires.[31] Gender could be troubled and disturbed; it could be *bent*. But bending always presupposed a preexistent entity – a historical culture that preceded it as a set of repertoires, roles, signs, penalties and social pressures. One could not autonomously select or invent one's gender whole cloth.

Of central importance, gender performativity was a politics whose concerns went beyond feminist confrontation with patriarchy to include gay, lesbian, bi, trans and queer resistance to what Butler called a "system of compulsory heterosexuality".[32] This innovation in feminist politics – away from the female sex to a coalition of nonconforming and marginalized sexual identities – in turn, generated internal rifts.[33] As the political theorist Wendy Brown pithily articulated these fault lines in the title of a 2015 talk: is the identity of women to be "dissolved or defended?"[34]

Suddenly, feminism was not just about women anymore. As with feminism more generally, one can recognize in this map a strong ethical dimension. This occurs as individuals and groups whose experience was one of political, social and psychological repression, fear and stigmatization step into the light of the public square and claim a sense of self. The politics of "coming out of the closet", for instance, is experienced not only as liberatory but also as an escape from a prior existence that is suffocating to one's very sense of existence. It would be a grave mistake to underestimate the sense-making and ethically magnetic powers of this political culture.

Nevertheless, the inclusion of those who were conventionally and biologically males at birth (either as part of the gay movement or as transwomen) likewise led to divisions. Many of the institutions and policies of first- and second-wave feminism – from the Seven Sisters colleges to Planned Parenthood and Title IX – had been set up as exclusively servicing the female sex. But now a question emerged: were these very same institutions progressive or regressive if they remained non-inclusive on the basis of biology? Should feminists continue to support female-only access to schools, sports, healthcare, and so on? Feminist polarization in these debates has turned into what is sometimes called gender-inclusive feminists arguing for access versus trans-exclusionary feminists advocating a retention of the older battlelines.

All of this has occurred, moreover, against the backdrop of a significant mobilization around what has been dubbed "choice feminism".[35] According to this ideological mutation, whatever a woman chooses in the context of a set of contractual, market relationships simply *is* feminism. As the singer-songwriter, Lana Del Rey, succinctly put it: "For me, a true feminist is someone who is a woman who does exactly what she wants".[36] In this way, the retrenchment around traditional sex divides was blended with right libertarian themes of individual autonomy. Paradoxically, from the choice feminist perspective, one might even say it is not "patriarchy" so long as a woman chooses it.

In popular culture, the proliferation of "Girl Boss" slogans, social-media influencer culture, Barbie aesthetics, and female entrepreneurial empowerment, all offered routes of return to the purportedly infantilizing and objectifying styles and behaviours that first- and second-wave feminists had sought to overcome. In another odd reversal of history, the very incursion into these career spaces was only made possible by the advance of the earlier movements in the first place. If choice feminism was not the dominant form of sexual politics at the beginning of the twenty-first century, it was certainly endemic.

Perhaps the intense confusion generated by feminist ideology is not only a function of its revolutionary power, as well as its liquid mutations and hybridizations, but also because it poses fundamental questions about the intersection of ideology as cultural and the human body. We already examined, in Chapter 1, Clifford Geertz's thesis that humans are "in physical terms . . . an unfinished animal" only made whole "through culture".[37] Yet feminism challenges to what extent cultural meanings might also saturate or enter into feedback loops with biology. For example, if a woman is born female, but then for cultural reasons eats less, allows her muscles to atrophy, waxes her androgenic hair, and so forth, to what degree has culture entered into biology? Or, conversely, are the embodied realities of biology – reproductive and hormonal – of consequence to culture as an underlying, incomplete base? Is there a porousness here between culture and nature that some future iteration of the feminist debate might sort out?

Regardless how these questions are answered, feminism is

clearly capable of hybridization across the ideological spectrum. It follows that those who assume the cultural logic of feminism is a self-evident, linear arrow, shooting through history to hit some predetermined mark, are badly lost. Instead, feminism has always been a diverse and contested range of political cultures with many possible futures. All of this leads to an overwhelming question – not do we accept feminism *tout court*?, but, whose feminism ought to prevail?

9

The meaning of the Earth: the challenges of ecological politics

Green, or ecological ideology, locates its central animating concern outside of the human community in nature and especially the interlocking ecosystems that crisscross the Earth. No doubt there are many competing forms of ecological politics – some which decentre human life more radically than others. But the unique magnetic force experienced by the multiple followers of this map is largely due to the importance it ascribes not only to plants and animals, but also to lakes, rivers, mountains, forests, seas, and all the other habitats that serve as home to living creatures. For green politics, the planet is centrally significant.

This chapter starts by reconstructing the ethical and meaning-making resources of green ideology, which originated in nineteenth-century romanticism and its rejection of the Enlightenment's picture of nature as a mechanics. This critique of a machine-like cosmos was pioneered not only by romantic poets but also by writers such as Henry David Thoreau, who carried out radical new experiments in living. A diffuse ethos derived from these various figures subsequently seeped into competing ideologies from across the political spectrum, creating various fusions that continue to confound the dualism of left versus right.

In what follows, I establish the liquidity of green politics, which, like feminism, is not a solid structural object that can be cleanly taxonomized as "on the left". Instead, it is a cultural map that is creatively adopted by an almost dizzying array of rival perspectives. These include the more strenuously anti-industrial politics of deep ecologists, counterculture hippies and pastoral conservatives, as well as the incremental and reform-minded approaches of eco-progressives and right libertarians. Lastly, there are various politics of ecological emergency that have intermixed with both socialist and fascist ideology. Thus, a cultural approach explodes the myth of a monumental green politics that is reducible to "tree huggers" and "environmental activists". To remain within these culture war clichés is not only to block true understanding of one's own time but also to obscure the conflicting sources of meaning that often inform and complicate one's very own politics.

VISIONS OF NATURE: MECHANISTIC VERSUS EXPRESSIVE

The ideologies stemming from the early Enlightenment were often oblivious to the possibility that nature bore any significance beyond serving as a resource for human development. To take a prominent example, consider the way in which Locke persistently referred to nature in his *Second Treatise* as a "waste" and insisted: "land that is left wholly to nature, that hath no improvement of pasturage, tillage, or planting, is called, as indeed it is, *waste*".[1] For Locke – and countless followers of his map – material nature only gained value when it was brought into the human economy through individual labour. This act converted nature from the condition of primordial "waste" into a privately-owned commodity ready for exchange or sale on a market.

Similarly, in the writings of Marx, nature was initially defined by economic scarcity. The natural world needed to be mastered by humans in order to produce the economic abundance that was a precondition for emancipation. Thus, Marx wrote that "just as the savage must wrestle with nature, in order to satisfy his wants ... so civilized man ... must do [the same] in all forms of society and under all possible modes of production". Indeed, the "realm of freedom" for Marx necessitated that "nature" be "brought under ... common control".[2] Historically, this culminated in "modern industry" and its "industrial armies" that "accomplished wonders far surpassing Egyptian pyramids, Roman aqueducts, and Gothic cathedrals", opening the way to a communist revolution.[3] In classical Marxism, nature was a site of struggle for increased material control, technological progress and freedom.

By contrast, ecological politics draws on romanticism's rejection of instrumental and economistic views of nature. The more radical the green politics, the more vigorous the ethical demand for a conversion away from the treatment of nature as simply a material basis for human needs. Instead, on the romantic view, nature embodies various intrinsic and expressive goods that go beyond human instrumentalization.

Of course, as is widely known, beginning in the late eighteenth-century, romantic artists and thinkers rejected the Enlightenment's vaunting of reason and its attendant idea of humans as rationalistic animals. Instead, the romantics insisted on the importance of the expressive features of human life.[4] As part of this, a key contrast emerged between the Enlightenment's view of nature as an impersonal mechanical system and the romantic vision of nature as expressive of deeper meanings. Where certain currents of the Enlightenment represented nature as a Newtonian apparatus of demystified causal relations (susceptible to instrumental control), romantic thinkers instead interpreted it as a source of meaning never to be exhausted by scientific description.

Indeed, on the romantic view, poetic language was necessary to encountering reality, while mathematics and the natural sciences could lead to distortions when taken as exclusively disclosing reality. In order to better understand this key claim, it is worth pondering Walt Whitman's short poem from 1865, "When I heard the learn'd astronomer". In this poem, the narrator describes a growing alienation before a purely mathematized and material idea of the cosmos offered by a scientific lecturer:

> When I heard the learn'd astronomer,
> When the proofs, the figures, were ranged in columns
>   before me,
> When I was shown the charts and diagrams, to add, divide,
>   and measure them,
> When I sitting heard the astronomer where he lectured with
>   much applause in the lecture-room,
> How soon unaccountable I became tired and sick,
> Till rising and gliding out I wander'd off by myself,
> In the mystical moist night-air, and from time to time,
> Look'd up in perfect silence at the stars.[5]

What we see in Whitman's poem – which sits as a counterpart or even replacement language for the theories of the scientific astronomer – is the need for deeper linguistic capacities to fully perceive nature. The astronomer's "charts and diagrams" not only fail to capture the whole of nature, but something in the very drive to "add, divide, and measure" closes off the path to a deeper relationship with it. The mode of scientific calculation frustrates the contemplative appreciation of nature. To set the balance right, the narrator abandons the lecture room into the "mystical moist night-air" and the "silence" of the stars. Even the form of Whitman's poem expresses a contemplative whole (in a single sentence that refuses to segment itself with a period), presenting itself as the foil to the atomistic analysis of Newtonianism. Poetics, in other words, and not mathematization, becomes integral to encountering nature.

Thus, nature was not simply a bundle of material causes and resources that could serve as means to different ends. As the American naturalist, John Muir, put it: one had to reject the view that "whales" were little more than "storehouses of oil".[6] Rather, nature exceeded any person's attempt to treat it like a tool. The cost of reducing nature to an instrument was to become separated from one's own sources of regeneration and happiness. Nature, then, had value as a contemplative good (whose sole purpose was to behold and marvel) beyond material uses. Politically speaking, this cleared the path for various ecological ideologies to argue that nature needed to be preserved, intrinsically valued, and even left alone in a state of wildness. Nature was no "waste". Its abundance defied human understanding.

WALDEN'S NATURE ETHOS

The interpretation of nature articulated by romanticism – together with its American counterpart, transcendentalism – helped inspire a diffuse *ethos* or loose set of identity traits, customs, convictions and practices. At the level of everyday experience, people influenced by this ethos frequently perceive nature as restorative and spiritually fulfilling (as opposed to, say, a site of Darwinian struggle and violence). But it has also spurred the development of an entire range of concrete practices said to be in harmony with nature's goodness

– from organic farming and composting to backpacking and "living off the grid".

It is this nature ethos that, albeit to dramatically varying degrees, has been adopted by ideological partisans across the spectrum. Even if only begrudgingly or covertly, a nature ethos colours nearly every cultural milieu, to some degree transforming modern identity. Very few, after all, feel comfortable parroting as if it were a neutral, sober fact Locke's definition of nature as "waste" (even as our many ideological cultures continue to straddle the newer and older modes).

One way to understand Henry David Thoreau's massive impact on later ecological politics is precisely as giving a classic account of this ethic in his masterwork from 1854, *Walden; or, Life in the Woods*. Thoreau's experiment in living continues to attract people from rival ideologies even as most of his contemporary readers deradicalize his call for abandoning society and returning to nature. Certainly, Thoreau's own life of simplicity living on Walden Pond for two years was expressive of a kind of primitive nature utopianism, attempting subsistence largely outside of the market and the state.

Much of *Walden* summarized the practical dimensions of simple living, growing one's own food and building and maintaining one's own shelter (Thoreau's famous cabin). But Thoreau's writing was also saturated by an intense attention to the rhythms, beauty and greater permanence of the natural world in contrast to modern society. As Thoreau, put it: "I went to the woods because I wished to live deliberately, to front only the essential facts of life, and see if I could not learn what it had to teach".[7] Nature's first and most enduring lesson was: "simplicity, simplicity, simplicity!" or an increasing ability to adopt asceticism as an alternative to capitalism's call for indefinite economic growth, material accumulation and technological innovation.[8] As Thoreau polemically observed: "men think that it is essential that the Nation have commerce, and export ice, and talk through a telegraph, and ride thirty miles an hour" but the result of all of this was that "we do not ride on the railroad; it rides upon us".[9]

This famous maxim from *Walden* is central to understanding Thoreau's articulation of the nature ethic. Where modern people believed they were in control and dominating the surrounding order, Thoreau detected a subtle reversal. Humans in the act of technological control and mediation were often cut off from deeper spiritual sources, losing a sense of purpose. "The mass of men lead lives of quiet desperation", he wrote.[10] The technology individuals employed to control and change the world changed them – robbing them of participation in the more enduring patterns of the natural world. *Walden*'s underlying aim was to reestablish the modern person's communion with nature at this deeper level.

Like Marxism, *Walden* implied that modern political life was characterized by alienation. Unlike Marxism, the crisis was ethical and ecological. Nature, on Thoreau's account, was already a good and superabundant space for dwelling prior to technological modernization. Where classical Marxism called for an acceleration through industrial capitalism and the generation of material abundance, Thoreau instead questioned the pace of growth and consumption. The experiment in living in *Walden* pointed to enduring themes of the nature ethos and later green politics: satisfaction with less, sustainability and anti-materialism.

I shall return to how various aspects of this nature ethos can fuse with the major ideological maps (including liberal capitalism and socialism). But for now, the point is that Thoreau helped introduce the disturbing notion that technology, as the rational control of nature, did not in fact accomplish a straightforward emancipation nor a satiation of desire. To the contrary, one ended up fettered to a defective ethic of rational control – one that appeared to gain dominion over nature, but untethered modern society from healthier patterns of consumption and need.

In doing so, technological society gained a temporary and immediate victory over nature at the cost of losing control over human acquisitive desire. This could eventually unleash catastrophic disequilibria in nature as ecosystems were strained to meet humanity's industrial "needs" on a mass scale. A cultural pattern therefore penetrated the natural world such that it was no exaggeration to say that human activity altered the unfolding processes of nature. Thoreau's maxim, "we do not ride on the railroad; it rides upon us", can be interpreted as prophetic of countless human-made ecological catastrophes where technological control turns against its users in the form of dustbowls, nuclear hazard zones, polluted streams, unbreathable air, warming climate and floods.

Later ecological thinkers went beyond Thoreau in theorizing this drive to dominate nature as instigating a chain of unintended consequences. As technology on a planetary scale drew more of nature under human power, nature was said to return each time with greater volatility. Such philosophical themes were echoed, for example, in Martin Heidegger's critique of technology.[11] More recently, Hartmut Rosa observed: "the endeavor to expand our share of the world, to bring the forests and the mountains under our control" leads to reversals by which that very "exploited segment of world" became "hard, barren, even downright hostile".[12] The drive to control nature, as Rosa powerfully argued, unleashes greater episodes of uncontrollability. A disordered self, spurring human economy and politics to unreasonable ends, eventually produces a disordered and intractable nature. The popular notion of the "Anthropocene" – or a geological era characterized by human alteration of the Earth's ecosystems – captures something of this paradoxical process of simultaneously heightened control and loss of control.

AGAINST INDUSTRIALIZATION: DEEP ECOLOGISTS, HIPPIES AND PASTORALISTS

The proliferation of the nature ethos, its cultural meanings and practices, can take more intense or diluted form. But this should not hide the fact that both radical greens and more reformist movements have been influenced by it. Often the more radical the movement, the sharper its denouncement and rebuke of industrialization and modern patterns of politics and economy. The latter is certainly true of a cluster of radical green ideologies that have demanded immediate alternatives to the major ideologies and their dependence on modern technology.

A particularly dramatic strain of the radicalization of green ideology is the case of "deep ecology" championed by the Norwegian philosopher, Arne Næss. Næss received considerable attention for proposing that an authentic ecological politics would need to move beyond all the existing traditions in the West, including mere calls for "environmental" stewardship. The latter were complicit in what Næss called "anthropocentrism" – or the view that all value and significance centred on human purposes and well-being. The result of anthropocentrism was a "shallow" ecology that inevitably instrumentalized and degraded the very environment it claimed to protect. Instead, a new politics needed to be forged that was eco- or bio-centric (in which the natural world was accorded its own value). Næss's polemic against "environmentalism" was precisely that it did not live up to a deep ecological outlook that saw in nature its own intrinsic worth.[13]

Deep ecology created support for all kinds of radical possibilities that remain on the far horizon of radical green politics today, including: the search for decentred and biocentric forms of community; the prizing of non-human species (including animal rights); the replacement of the modern food system with sustainability and veganism; and the planning of a smaller human population. In this manner, Næss might be thought of as a particularly uncompromising radicalization of the nature ethic.

But deep ecologists were not the only ideological group insisting on an immediate rejection of mass-scale industrial economies and politics as usual. The Sixties counterculture popularized many of the themes of the romantic nature ethic (once the reserve of elite poets and intellectuals) while also mobilizing small-scale utopian and pastoral communes. If once only a few visionaries, like William Wordsworth, had made a spiritual pilgrimage – "lonely as a cloud" to dance "with the daffodils" in nature – now an entire youth movement styled itself as *flower children*.[14] For many hippies, nature was the key site of spiritual, personal and political awakening.

The so-called "back-to-nature" movement of the hippies included everything from organizing communes and farmer's markets, to massive rural music festivals and anti-consumerist nature sports. Likewise, many of the fruits of Mother Nature – from marijuana to psilocybin – were to be liberalized and treated non-moralistically as part of raising consciousness. These countercultural experiments could be difficult to categorize ideologically, often lumped together under the banner of the "New Age", they might be fused with anarchism, eco-socialism, progressive liberalism, and even hints of pastoral conservatism. Later, many of the counter culture's avant-garde and New Age practices would be absorbed into capitalist and libertarian ideological culture (for example, REI, organic "whole" foods, and "micro-dosing").

Particular to the hippies, however, was an interpretation of the nature ethic as both pacifistic and erotically sensualist (Thoreau had still been culturally immersed in New England Puritanism). Reconnecting with nature revealed to hippies an Edenic space existing prior to society's moralisms, industrial chemicals, phony wars, and traditional taboos on sex and narcotics. Although some of these themes were recognizable from Rousseau's philosophy, the hippies rejected the latter's interpretation of nature as Spartan or militaristic in its virtues and insisted it was peacenik. For the hippies, industrial and consumer society represented a calamitous fall from a peaceful and spiritually fulfilling, ecological innocence. As Joni Mitchell (one of many hippie musicians stylizing as natural) summarized this catastrophe: "They paved paradise / And put up a parking lot".[15]

Sometimes hippieism could blur imperceptibly with themes borrowed from pastoral conservatism. The latter was arguably the oldest form of ecological ideology – drawing on nostalgia in Europe for medievalism, as well as romanticism's critique of industrialization, it advocated a return to agrarian society. Preindustrialism, according to pastoral-conservative ecologists, was a time of greater sustainability and harmony with nature. Unlike countercultural pastoralism, this politics fused a nature ethic with traditional religion, folk morality and a re-enchantment of the cosmos. The poet Wendell Berry, for example, called for an ecological politics organized around a "love for local things, rising out of local knowledge and local allegiance".[16]

Yet pastoral conservatives also faced similar questions to those looming over deep ecology and the hippie counterculture: was this politics viable? Could it be achieved at any scale? What did transition to the new ecological society look like? Pastoral, agrarian idylls might resonate deeply with huge numbers of people – expressing a homey version of the nature ethic – but they also appeared unattainable for communities dependent on industrial economies and lacking the material basis or knowledge for making life on a farm real. Indeed, even the rural communities in much of the modern world had been rendered into vast industrial enterprises and not quaint towns nurturing "local things".

Perhaps for this reason, the most powerful articulators of conservative pastoralism have always been imaginative writers and poets.

For example, the fantasy novels of J. R. R. Tolkien contain conservative pastoral and nostalgically medieval ecological themes. The chief protagonists – Hobbits – live a cosy, sustainable existence of crafts and farming, while Elves wander in harmony with the forests and the very trees speak amiably about caring for other creatures. Indeed, in Tolkien's novels only humanoid monsters (the Orcs) engage zealously in activities that look vaguely like the mass industrial devastation of nature, as they occupy deserted wastelands where smoke-like clouds choke the sky, and no flower or green thing ever grows.

LIBERAL-GREEN REFORMISM

Despite their formidable symbolic power, both the pastoral and hippie interpretations of green ideology have remained more a daydream for millions of people than an attainable reality. Larger mobilizations have instead occurred around calls to reform industrialization. A prominent example is the fusion between progressive ideology and the various themes of the nature ethic brought to public attention via the counterculture and socially liberal journalism. For example, Mitchell's anthemic folk song – "Big Yellow Taxi" – was appreciated far outside hippie culture and made clear reference to Rachel Carson's *Silent Spring* published in 1962. Carson's exposé taught millions of readers about the detrimental side-effects of agribusiness's use of pesticides like DDT.[17] As part of this, a new ecological idea began circulating more widely in the popular discourse: the ecosystem.

An ecosystem was partly a scientific description of the interdependency of organisms in the natural environment. But it was also forged into an ideological concept capturing the interconnectedness of human society and nature. Strictly speaking, the welfare of humans and of nature was blurred and intertwined. The invisible ties binding the two were daily being discovered – in food systems and disease, industrial byproducts and climate, consumption and sustainability, and many more.

The power of Carson's writing was to make the politics of ecosystems vividly clear for readers by describing pesticides detrimental effects on humans and the bird population. Hauntingly, Carson imagined a cataclysmic, future "silent spring", with no birdsong. In this way, the human polity itself was relocated for countless readers as inside a larger web of life (the ecosystem). The map of green ideology expanded to straddle the human/nature divide.

For left-leaning liberals and social democrats, the goal had long been to stabilize capitalism through a government securing the welfare and economic security necessary for citizens to exercise individual autonomy. A growing awareness of ecosystems now made a new fusion possible. Namely, added to the traditional items of welfare (social security, food, living wages, and so on) was the regulation of human activity to put it in harmony with the surrounding environment. The health of the ecosystem was ingredient in the flourishing of persons, making it a part of individual liberty. Freedom from the negative externalities of an unchecked, laissez-faire industrial capitalism – which in turn undermined human agency by creating hazardous and possibly deadly environmental toxins and pollutants – was integral to the progressive agenda.

In terms of public policy, this meant the state had a legitimate role to play in implementing regulations that controlled the profiteering of the private sector and monitored the health of the environment to avert various crises of the commons. For example, corporations might find it more "efficient" to dump toxic byproducts into the local river. Entities set up to monitor profit-seeking businesses (such as, in the United States, the Environmental Protection Agency) were a fusionist expression of ecology and social liberalism. They did not aim to abolish industrialization and technological capitalism, but to reform it.

Likewise, the progressive version of wilderness preservation was not merely of pedagogical value, but also geared towards aesthetic well-being (harkening back to *Walden*). More recently, progressivism's joining of ecological and human welfare, has inspired talk of a "Green New Deal", whose advocates hope to tackle inequality and the environmental crisis at the same time through "large-scale federal investment" in green jobs and technologies. This is conceived as "saving capitalism from itself".[18] Thus, we have a vision of green social democracy that might blend into democratic socialist initiatives as well.

Yet, in a replay of earlier twentieth-century polarization, social liberals also faced resistance from inside the broader liberal tradition from those who believed laissez-faire markets would engender the technological innovation necessary to save the planet from ecological disaster. Green libertarians conceded that ecological degradation was a problem (perhaps a "negative externality") of modern, industrialized economies. But, they instead argued the best way to handle the problem was via markets that inspired technological innovation (for example, Tesla) and quasi-markets that restructured individual incentives (for example, carbon credits).

Right-libertarian or neoliberal ecology pushed to privatize the environmental crisis by devolving it onto personal responsibility and consumer choices. The resolution was not social organization or governmental action but individual initiative. For example, libertarians devised the culture of shopping green – with consumer products like electric cars, organic food, solar panels, xeriscaping, and other sustainability items selected by individuals with a preference for "saving the planet". What made these actions distinctly right libertarian was the rejection of social democratic or other communal action. Instead, individuals inside a free market were the only ones who could efficiently respond to the ecological crisis by recycling, building green, composting, starting a green business, and so on.

ECOLOGICAL EMERGENCIES: ECO-SOCIALISM VERSUS ECO-FASCISM

Although early Marxism is sometimes criticized by greens for its focus on generating material surpluses via industrialization, it has in recent decades also fused with ecological ideology. This eco-Marxism sees environmental devastation as a further crisis of capitalism and perhaps even a central driver of revolutionary change. Marxists like Mark Fisher have argued that the new crisis is not chiefly one of proletariat radicalization but instead an environmental catastrophe on a scale that gradually engulfs and undermines the entirety of societal well-being. An event like climate change and the massive loss of longstanding ecosystems (laid to waste by extreme weather, floods, fires, droughts, and extinction) might overcome the widespread perception that capitalism is a realistic way to organize modern society.

Indeed, on this view, the increasing experience of trauma around climate disasters might push people en masse towards new ideological forms that finally leave capitalism behind.[19] In other words, eco-socialists believe that Marx was correct to posit that capitalism was unstable, but incomplete in his theory. The revolutionary crisis is not primarily brought on by the immiseration of the proletariat, but by the ecological undermining of the viability of capitalism as a whole. The only way to overcome planetary collapse is to achieve post-capitalism.

However, insofar as Marxism still relies on overcoming natural scarcity through technological innovation it remains unclear how such green futures avoid many of the problems plaguing capitalism. If green technology is supposed to resolve the dual crises of scarcity and ecology, then ironically eco-socialism ends up endorsing a version of the libertarian claim that technological innovation provides the solution as opposed to exacerbating the situation. Regardless, it is clear that green ideology is liquid enough to blend with even the most techno-utopian of ideologies: from relatively orthodox Marxism to libertarianism.

An alternative map of eco-socialism, which does not rely on Marx's optimism about mass industrialization, was articulated by Murray Bookchin. Bookchin's "municipal" or civic approach gave a central role to a certain kind of city not as the opposite of nature but as its complement and culmination. The city–nature dichotomy was rejected by Bookchin who insisted that the right kind of ecological city was at one and the same time on a "human scale" and a "natural scale".[20] These cities would need to include walkability and public transport (mostly eliminating cars) as well as localized food and economic systems. Cities that operated hyper-locally could be sensitive to their immediate environment, using materials for living derived from them. Bookchin, therefore, called for a "dramatic variety of communal forms – marked by architectural and industrial adaptations to the local ecosystems", from semi-arid grasslands to forests and swamps.[21] Energy, too, would reflect local conditions and draw on solar, tidal, wind, and other resources accordingly.

From a cultural perspective, it is again important to emphasize that ecological meanings can effortlessly graft themselves onto a politics that synthesizes small-scale utopian socialism with a left-wing version of Tocqueville's civic republicanism. Although

Bookchin's politics are difficult to imagine being realized (in a world where few such cities exist even in germinal form), his theory nonetheless remains more culturally sensitive than the crude forms of economistic scientism that currently predominate. As Thomas More famously quipped, one might wish, rather than expect to see such utopian politics gain momentum.

Unfortunately, what remains far easier to imagine under current cultural conditions is the formation of an ecological, ethnic nationalism and even eco-fascism. These ideological maps hold that the best response to environmental catastrophe is not international cooperation but rather the reassertion ofborders and ethnic communities. The polity becomes a kind of life-raft or citadel against the ravages of climate and eco-disasters. Part of the role of eco-fascist government is defined as protecting the ethnos from succumbing to climate refugees permitted by liberals to overload the national life-raft.

Indeed, eco-fascists dating back to the twentieth century have fused themes of ethnic purity and environmental preservation.[22] The ethnic and racial group, was seen by early eco-fascists, as having a unique relationship to the living space of the natural world. Wilderness preservation was in this way bound together with ethnic preservation. Following Carl Schmitt, eco-fascists today might install a dictatorial leader by declaring a state of emergency brought on by an ecological crisis or by massive displacement of climate refugees. In a parallel case to eco-Marxism, the emergency might "go green".

Fascism in general, as an ideological map, has many problems discussed in Chapter 5. But from an ecological perspective, it is unclear if a non-global solidarity, like fascism, can really fend off a planetary crisis. Each ethnic group attempting to make impregnable fortresses out of their countries may only serve to reveal the futility of this project. The most recent ecological disasters have made all sovereignties weak and porous. Not only do displaced persons press at borders, but the environment itself, overwhelms and reshapes the land without respecting frontiers. Clouds, fires, floods and pollution barrel over national lines. It is possible that ideological maps, unable to achieve global cooperation, will also be helpless when confronting such situations.

Regardless how one decides to chart the ecological crisis, green thought poses the novel problem that in the case of nature there is no interpretation-free way to apprehend it. To this must also be added that our ideological cultures seem to porously pass over into natural systems and set off chains of cause and effect far beyond anyone's control. One cannot help but conclude that one enduring insight of green politics is that the political world and the Earth are not so easily separable as first appeared manifest.

Conclusion: the age of ideologies

> It is very difficult if not impossible in this life to achieve certainty about these questions, at the same time, it is utterly feeble not to use every effort in testing the available theories ... to select the best and most dependable theory that human intelligence can supply, and use it as a raft to ride the seas of life.
>
> Plato, *Phaedo* 85c–d[1]

We live in an age of ideologies. This political reality is in a strange way given, even fated. None of us can help or change the epoch any more than a medieval peasant could leap out of the cosmic chain of being. An age of ideologies will surely come to an end, but no one knows when or how. To grasp by what cultural mutation it might be superseded, would already imply the first dawning of that future time. When such a new reality is visible it will already, in some senses, be upon us.

No living person can see beyond an age of ideologies because it consumes the current horizon of the visible. Indeed, as these pages have shown time and again, to believe one can do without ideology is simply to naively extend its domain.[2] Even when individuals disavow ideology, or seem unable to coherently reconstruct their own beliefs, they nonetheless remain encircled by its meanings, which are embodied in institutions, patterns of action and practices.[3] Ideology is never just in our heads, but has built our social reality. Its many maps govern the contours of our world.

As in the ancient Jewish story of the Tower of Babel, ideologies are like spires which humans raise relentlessly towards the sky in an effort to achieve a God's eye view – to loom above history and resolve the anguished problems of human injustice, violence, fighting, oppression and disorder. Those who make the effort to climb the stairs of a particular tradition's Tower of Babel, find not only various weak points in the structure along the way, but also (as in the famous paintings by Pieter Bruegel) the pinnacle unfinished. Every ideological tower reaches a point of inarticulacy where it is permanently in ruins even as it is being built.

An age of ideologies is an age of spectacular towers that appear monolithic from the ground level but when they reach the clouds are still works in progress. The very effort to build such ambitious monoliths, which are the work of many hands over untold generations, isolates us from the inhabitants of rival towers. Similar to the story of Babel, the result of the ambition to build a tower to heaven is confusion on Earth, as competing groups no longer understand each other's speech and fall into a babble of tongues. Whenever we inhabit such siloed towers and make no effort to leave them – not even in the imagination and through dialogue – we do not understand the point of view of our neighbours who are aloft in a nearby tower of their own. We can only look across from windows at each other's strange faces in silence.

The various ideological languages make us strangers who do not understand one another's utterances. The very tower that was supposed to be a symbol of monolinguistic unity, divides and isolates us. More confusing still, the different ideological lexicons exist within the same natural languages. So, commonly used English words like "freedom", "equality", "the people", "democracy", "order", "justice", "solidarity", and "authority" can mean completely different things. People are speaking foreign ideological languages without realizing it because they are speaking the same natural language.

Of course, most people do not grasp their own predicament because they have allowed themselves to be taken captive by only one ideological language. They are ideologically monolingual and cannot find the exit to their own tower. A cultural approach offers temporary escape from our towers by granting us greater fluency and multilingual ability. The tools to achieve ideological multilingualism include informal dialogue, long-form interviews, careful reading, historical research and ethnographic immersion.[4] To truly hear ideologies speak in their own voice, we need approaches that are sensitive to their meanings.

In this sense, the goal of this book has been to allow readers (even if only momentarily) to be less in the thrall of their own ideology and grasp why someone else's ideology is attractive. This is, after all, the general ideological predicament of our time – all of us must hazard our lives by either explicitly pledging allegiance or tacitly participating in some ideology. Although our maps are certainly different, we share this existential conundrum.

IDEOLOGY AND THE PROBLEM OF RELATIVISM

For the millions of people who are currently lost in ideology, political debate with opponents often consists of little more than bald assertions, condescension, haughtiness and moralizing. From deep inside a particular map, it appears self-evident that the world is necessarily "thus and so". Anyone unable to see by the blinding light of one's own ideological sun is benighted, irrational, wicked or otherwise false. All that is left to do is summarize one's obviously righteous creed and post it for public admonition (perhaps on a picket sign, bumper sticker, or T-shirt).

When this happens, political debate becomes fruitless. Opposing sides yell with a certainty that betrays the profound threat of a gnawing doubt from inside, that must be hidden first and foremost from oneself. As in *Hamlet*, this ideological environment is one in which "the lady doth protest too much" – and all of us are the lady. Dialogue then appears futile and Schmitt's notion that all politics is a standoff between friends and enemies begins to gain ground, infiltrating many of the ideological maps. Fascism and authoritarianism thrive in a world where dialogue makes no difference and everything consists of raw power struggles.

Unfortunately, empiricist political science only exacerbates this situation. Limiting the role of reason to merely describing existing belief systems – and perhaps correlating them with other variables and bits of social reality – it tacitly reduces political convictions to a mere act of the will, an irrational leap towards a given worldview. The ethical and political authority of any given ideology depends on a will to power; a certain kind of Nietzscheanism is conceded at the philosophical level. Thus, political science appears ethically and ideologically neutral but this is an illusion. It instead inadvertently teaches a soft relativism that goes hand in hand with a supposedly ideology-free empiricism.

But, in reality, empiricism does not even meet its own modest standard of describing the world. A first-person, cultural approach to ideology reveals that mainstream social science runs against ordinary self-understanding (what philosophers call "phenomenology") insofar as people for the most part hold their political convictions because they think of them as true and ethically binding. When social scientists describe ideological beliefs as merely serving a subjective function of legitimating authority or correlating with supposedly more objective "data", they are unknowingly contradicting the actual experience of ideology as ethically and politically true.

At the same time, when it comes to ideological truth the stakes are enormous. Every one of these maps has been the site of massive wars, incarcerations, political assassinations, poverty, deprivation and loss. Both adherents and foes have died on the imagined cartographies and strange terrains of ideology. Flags have been raised over the heaping piles of the dead that decompose and manure the ideological ground from which further ideas like *les fleurs du mal* grow.

This brings us to a fundamental set of questions concerning a cultural approach to ideology: namely, from what perspective do we pronounce objective judgements on ideology? Is not every possible criticism already an expression of another, rival ideological system? And does this not make every ideology equally valid from its own perspective? In other words, does not a cultural approach also bottom out into a subjective treatment of ideology? This is the spectre of relativism, and I now must scare it off.

HOW TO ARGUE ABOUT IDEOLOGY 1: EXTERNAL CRITICISMS

A cultural or interpretive approach to ideology is also always critical.[5] All along I have been practicing this philosophically critical form of inquiry but it is time to state explicitly how this works. There are at least two general clusters of objective criticism that interpretive philosophy makes possible through its attention to ideologies as cultural maps.

To begin with, since all ideologies involve a mixture of some descriptive and enactive or worldmaking claims, one can appeal to the authority of the natural sciences or some other range of relevant facts (when these are available) to show that an ideology is unable to account for significant swaths of reality. This should not at all be confused for the claim that ideological controversy can finally be resolved through the authority of science. It cannot. But philosophically defensible ideologies must be able to square with the best account of the natural sciences. This may not get us very far in the domain of political conflict, but it is also not totally bereft of critical bite.

But there is a much deeper and more subtle form of ideological critique, generated by the very philosophical commitments of a cultural or interpretive approach. This is a line of argument that I have pursued throughout these pages, with the concept of being "lost in ideology", in which one mistakes cultural maps for the naturally and scientifically given account of the world. Because ideologies always exceed simply descriptive claims and evoke an ethically magnetic vision of what is significant or meaningful, they are never simply factual but rallying calls to mass-scale worldmaking. Indeed, even the more descriptive propositions of an ideological theory are often in a complex relationship with social reality and can be mobilized for world-building purposes.[6]

Interpretive philosophy, therefore, has never been a neutral observer on the scene. While not establishing any one ideology as definitively true, it nevertheless de-naturalizes and negates all ideologies that wear the cloak of scientism or naturalism. There are too many examples of such criticisms in the foregoing pages to summarize them here. But I might all-too-briefly note that my approach calls into question and even negates ideological maps that present themselves as simply historical mechanics or brute facts. It does so by revealing how ideologies are the result of creative interpretive activity – dense matrices of meaning that are historically born and undergo continual modification and differentiation.

For example, where natural-rights liberals like Locke claimed to simply describe a state of nature, they in fact helped create a world in which such things as rights and liberal postulates appeared natural and commonsensical. The map of liberalism made a world in which liberalism became obviously true. Similarly, a cultural approach invalidates the vast multitudes of ideologies that claim to wield a scientific analysis for organizing society (such as most forms of utilitarianism, right libertarianism and many kinds of Marxism). Although White supremacist ideologies are objectionable for many reasons, they also run afoul of this interpretive insight as they fail to see their central concept of race as itself part of a cultural map (a "floating signifier" in Stuart Hall's memorable phrase). I could, of course, go on enumerating at great length the ways in which cultural interpretation discredits specific maps, but it would be better if readers returned to particular chapters to receive this analysis in detail.

The general philosophical point at present is that this kind of cultural criticism of ideology is ultimately subtractive. It eliminates certain ideological options and formations without being absorbed or trapped in any single tradition or map. Not unlike the practice of negative theology (in which theologians limit themselves to saying what God is *not*) so too an interpretive philosophical approach can objectively establish what a true ideology is *not*. It is not science. It is not a bare collection of facts. It is not data and numbers. It is not self-evident rationalism and commonsense. It is not realistic pragmatism, much less supernaturally given. A true ideology must be able to affirm and recognize its own cultural and historical nature. It must be able to self-narrate as an interpretive and worldmaking project. Any ideology unable to justify itself in these terms – because it makes a wild and illegitimate grab at pure "science", naturalism, or self-evident reason – is negated.

The question then becomes how one might adjudicate and decide between the rival forms of ideology that are still standing after this kind of cultural and interpretive critique has been conducted. Or is it the case that the problem of relativism returns insofar as the remaining options each appear equally true from their own perspective? This is where a second cluster of strategies for achieving objectivity and criticism in the realm of ideology becomes vital.

HOW TO ARGUE ABOUT IDEOLOGY 2: INTERNAL CRITICISMS

A second cluster of criticisms is internal to an agent's or tradition's self-understanding. By internal I mean two possibilities which are conceptually distinct but often overlap in reality: that is, not only internal to a given ideological tradition, but also internal to a particular person's self-understanding (which very often contains multiple ideological traditions and hybridizations, as well as other sources of meaning). Because an interpretive approach aims to faithfully capture an ideology's sense-making powers, it is also uniquely positioned to identify tensions internal to a given matrix of meaning.

One way this might be accomplished – evident throughout these pages – is by appealing to an ideal or authoritative articulator inside a tradition that can be used to correct less coherent versions that draw on the same concepts and meanings. For instance, the ordinary person who self-identifies as a "conservative" might assume this defence of tradition coheres easily with a commitment to laissez-faire markets. Yet the reconstruction of authoritative and ideally articulate figures within the conservative tradition, such as Edmund Burke, reveals a far more complex philosophical situation. In truth, the conservative notion of tradition is both conceptually and sociologically in tension with markets, which can reduce inherited authority and values to simply more instances of consumer choice (something already discussed in considerable detail).

At the same time, as we saw in the chapters on conservatism and right libertarianism, a philosophically authoritative figure to these traditions like Hayek very clearly shows that the liberal commitment to abstract principles is in tension with inherited deference to the status quo which can change with time and place. Conservatism is therefore philosophically incompatible with a steadfast commitment to libertarian individual property rights and markets. The ordinary attempt to fuse the two is objectively incoherent on its own terms.

In this way, cultural and historical sensitivity to an ideal or authoritative articulator can be used to gain critical leverage over an ideological tradition. Ordinary members of an ideology, when confronted with a more sophisticated account of their own commitments might experience a certain critical tension. Perhaps they believed they were the inheritors of a mere conservatism that peacefully coexisted with right libertarianism. But now they can see there is a problem. Burke's articulation of tradition is a more thorough and philosophically defensible formulation than their own. They then might correct to one of the more coherently articulated positions, or else attempt to resolve the conceptual contradiction in some other way by making an innovation. But the ideal articulator is an objective source of criticism insofar as it can be shown to constitute a philosophically superior theory on terms internal to an ideological map that a person already holds as binding.

Ideological maps are iterative. In any of the ideologies we have studied, one can objectively establish inferior and superior philosophical articulations of the same map. There is no problem of relativism internal to a tradition in which a shared framework can be used to determine better or worse in a variety of ways. When someone finds themselves pulled between two or more ideological maps or iterations this sometimes leads to conceptual innovation but often results instead in a crisis of belief. These dilemmas do not necessitate movement out of an ideological map, but they can cause internal disorientation within one's own cartography. A dramatic enough experience of disorientation might inspire particular individuals or even large groups to relocate or "convert" to some other ideological map altogether.

All the major ideologies experience internal tensions and dilemmas, and much of the foregoing chapters consisted of flagging such fault lines.[7] For example, Marxists cope with the problem of the working class becoming a bastion for conservative sentiment in many countries, instead of a revolutionary agent. Nationalists are bedeviled by how to establish a homogeneous sovereign culture against existing sources of heterogeneity. Feminists must grapple with whether the sex-versus-gender distinction ultimately negates or fulfills a politics that originated in the call to emancipate biological women. Multiculturalists negotiate the paradox of how deep diversity nonetheless coalesces in unity.

None of these lines of criticism is meant to be treated as conclusive. The point is instead to suggest how internal critique can do damage to an ideology on its own terms. The identification of such dilemmas – and the force of this criticism – depends on achieving ever greater interpretive clarity about a given map. If this is achieved, an ideology can be shown to be objectively inadequate or incoherent on its own terms. When no better version is offered, such inconsistencies might prove devastating.

Of course, most people in the world draw on multiple sources of meaning to guide their lives, not merely ideological but also biographical, ethical, religious, philosophical, literary, and otherwise. In cases where an ideology is combined or adopted conjointly with other sources, one might create critical leverage by highlighting how one set of meanings or distinct tradition challenges another. For instance, many Christians in the West currently identify with ethnic nationalism. But through cultural inquiry one might return with greater historical sensitivity to canonical articulations of Christian faith (say, for example, Jesus's Sermon on the Mount or Augustine's *De civitate Dei*) to call into question such ideological commitments. In another case, the rival sources of meaning might be Islamic, Jewish, Buddhist – or more secular sources of meaning like what Charles Taylor describes as the modern ethics of authenticity and affirmation of the ordinary.[8]

No doubt this latter point opens an enormously complex set of interpretive questions and controversies made all the more difficult by ideology's ability to engulf theology, philosophy, and any other source of meaning. But no matter how difficult, it also represents a real route to objective criticism. One set of beliefs can be shown to objectively contradict or cancel out another. Indeed, such a heightened interpretive encounter with one's own sources of meaning might lead an individual on a quest for discovery to see which convictions are most deeply held, and how their ideological maps require reform or even radical transformation.

Finally, as part of the appeal to existing commitments, there is also the question of the extent to which our emotional life and intuitions are pre-ideological or shaped by a given ideological matrix. Within ideological debate one might always appeal to a person's existing intuitions, emotional life, and experiences, to see if these are able to challenge their map. Is there some sense in which recurrent moods – for example, malaise within the economy, joy before nature, sadness before some loss or calamity – are in tension with an ideology? Marx and Thoreau are both certainly suggestive in different ways with their claims that modern society is characterized by mass alienation and desperation. Although these formidable minds did not think of it in this way, there might be something vitally important (even if beyond the range of the present study) in the notion that a given cultural map leads to unintended and undesirable socio-psychological states.

IDEOLOGY AND BEING HUMAN

Objectivity in the realm of ideology is comparative and provisional. This does not make it any less true. But it does mean there is something always open-ended and contestable in ideological controversy. There is no way to simply defeat an ideology with a single argument – logical or empirical. This is not the same as saying that logical and empirical considerations are unimportant. Rather logical clarity and empirical knowledge are indispensable. But no single arrow can slay the dragon of ideology. As worldmaking cultures, ideologies always extend beyond proofs and litmus tests by posing questions of significance, interpretation and meaning.

What is a significant or meaningful vision of society? This is not a question that can be answered by formal deduction, empirical testing, or mathematical reasoning alone. Even in the face of criticism, the followers of a given ideology can always draw on other parts of their tradition to attempt to resolve or address a dilemma. Interpretive philosophy, therefore, teaches a certain epistemic humility before ideological traditions. As Paul Ricoeur summarized this key point: "the critique of ideology is a task which we must always start, but which we cannot ever complete".[9]

But if ideologies are not vulnerable to a single *coup de grace*, it neither follows that they are invincible. Just the opposite: all the existing ideologies suffer from deep cuts. This does not render them all equal. Rather, the work of objectivity is comparative – requiring patient criticism and moving back and forth between rivals to see which ideology is more successful on the whole. Imagination and sense-making skills are essential. Without these, people are robbed of any ability to fruitfully and critically dialogue across ideologies.

The truth is that every person is in principle recruitable to any one of the ideological traditions – albeit for some the rival sources of meaning they draw upon will make it highly improbable and nearly unimaginable. But even in cases like White supremacy (where it seems no sane person of colour would willingly tread) there are complex forces at play. For example, in a White supremacist society, do Black police officers participate in enforcing racial caste at the level of practice if not belief? What about racial minorities adopting strategies to appear "Whiter" – in terms of cosmetics, dress and speech?

More disturbing still, is the possibility posed by Malcolm X of having internalized aspects of White supremacist belief as a Black person. In an oft-quoted speech from 1963 he suggested different mentalities of collaboration and resistance in the historical legacies of the "house Negro" versus the "field Negro" in the plantation South. The former, who worked in the house and enjoyed special privileges, often identified with and defended the "master" in ways that those suffering in the fields never dreamt of doing.[10] Malcolm's unsettling – but also ideologically profound – story suggests that meaning-making is so powerful a force in politics that it can even bewitch a small group of oppressed slaves into supporting the cause of the master.

Whatever we ultimately make of Malcolm's ideological parable, it is helpful in drawing our attention to the way that ideologies are perplexingly liquid and hotly contested. Any act of comprehension will require a highly sensitive and informed art of interpretation. But however difficult and thorny, this art of understanding may be, it is also necessary to grasping the modern predicament. To fail to see how individuals are always capable of converting into these various maps is itself a symptom of being ideologically dazed. It is to be cut off from the full drama of being human at the current moment.

An interpretive approach teaches a kind of humanistic sympathy when encountering ideology. This sympathy should never be mistaken for moral approval or sentimentalism. Rather, it involves a heightened awareness of the fact that humans are, as Geertz taught, makers of meaning who must spin out webs of significance no less than spiders their webs. We, too, are suspended in space and time by these complex, sometimes nearly invisible threads. We, too, catch and are caught in our own knots. Sometimes we fail to remember this, but interpretative consciousness like dew or sunlight can trace the outlines of our collective work and bring it into our field of vision. The problem of being human is not chiefly one of meaninglessness, but of the inescapability and even tangled overabundance of meaning.

So, our study of ideology has always been conducted at the margins and borders of ideology itself, where human creative, poetic and linguistic capacities take on different historical shapes in massive collective works. Among the greatest dangers in an age of ideologies is that this human factor will be forgotten. Our ideological map will swallow our entire perceptual field and make us unable to recognize the fellow human beings – fellow makers of meaning – living underneath.

At the centre of interpretive resistance to ideology is the awareness of a being whose meanings always exceed their own self-understandings. The point here is not to ally with a single ideology – say, liberalism and its affirmation of human rights. Rather, analogously to religion, a humanistic onlooker on ideology might hope for versions of the various maps that are more sensitive to this truth to prevail. After all, have not humanists long wished for more humane priests, pastors, imams, rabbis, and other authorities across the world's religions?

Similarly, in the sphere of ideology, we might favour those ideologies that made a humanistic turn. When it comes to liberalism, T. H. Green's positive conception of freedom might be praised over the scientistic libertarianism of Milton Friedman; when encountering socialism, Murray Bookchin's ethical municipalities over Stalin's economistic materialism; or when in dialogue with conservatism, Michael Oakeshott's anti-technocracy over Edmund Burke's sacralization of a single political community. This entire inquiry has contained a tacit affirmation of human beings above and beyond any one ideology. For those who have failed to detect this philosophical humanism there is a simple remedy. Namely, turn back the pages to set out again from where we started.

Notes

INTRODUCTION: IN SEARCH OF IDEOLOGY

1. See Charles Taylor, "Use and abuse of theory", in *Ideology, Philosophy and Politics*, ed. Anthony Parel (Waterloo: Wilfrid Laurier University Press, 1983), 39; Paul Ricoeur, "Can there be a scientific concept of ideology", in *Phenomenology and the Social Sciences: A Dialogue*, ed. Joseph Bien (The Hague: Martinus Nijhoff, 1978), 53.
2. Clifford Geertz, "Ideology as a Cultural System", in *The Interpretation of Cultures* (New York: Basic Books, 1973), 193.
3. Jorge Luis Borges, "Del rigor en la ciencia", *El Hacedor* (Madrid: Alianza Editorial, 1980), 143–4.
4. Richard Howe, "Notes on the Manhattan purchase", *Gotham Center for New York City History*, 27 June 2012; https://www.gothamcenter.org/blog/notes-on-the-manhattan-purchase.
5. Edwin Burrows and Mike Wallace, *Gotham: A History of New York City to 1898* (Oxford: Oxford University Press, 1999), 9.
6. For more on humans as meaning-makers, see Mark Bevir and Jason Blakely, *Interpretive Social Science* (Oxford: Oxford University Press, 2018), 1–64.
7. Clifford Geertz, "Thick description: toward an interpretive theory of culture", in *The Interpretation of Cultures*, 6.
8. Geertz, "Ideology as a cultural system", 220.
9. I am attempting, in my own words, to outline what Ricoeur referred to as an adequate hermeneutic "phenomenology of ideology"; see Ricoeur, "Can there be a scientific concept of ideology?", 44–59.
10. Michael Freeden, "Ideology and political theory", *Journal of Political Ideologies* 11:1(2006), 19.
11. See Jason Blakely, *We Built Reality: How Social Science Infiltrated Culture, Politics, and Power* (Oxford: Oxford University Press, 2020).
12. For example Richard Rorty, *Contingency, Irony, and Solidarity* (Cambridge: Cambridge University Press, 1989).
13. Charles Taylor, *A Secular Age* (Cambridge, MA: Harvard University Press, 2007), 423–72, 539–93.
14. William Shakespeare, *Richard II* in *The Norton Shakespeare: Histories*, eds S. Greenblatt *et al.* (New York: Norton, 2016) 2.4:7–15.

1 LIBERAL BY NATURE: VARIETIES OF CLASSICAL LIBERALISM

1. Louis Hartz, *The Liberal Tradition in America: An Interpretation of American Political Thought Since the Revolution* (New York: Harvest Book, 1952), 11.
2. Robert Frost, "Mending Wall", *The Poetry of Robert Frost*, ed. E. Lathem (New York: Holt, Rinehart & Winston, 1969), 33.
3. Hartz, *The Liberal Tradition in America*, 8.
4. Thomas Paine, *Common Sense* (Toronto: Broadview, 2004), 61.
5. John Locke, *The Second Treatise of Government* in *Political Writings*, ed. D. Wootton (Indianapolis, IN: Hackett, 2003), 273.
6. *Ibid.*, 314.
7. *Ibid.*, 312, 314.
8. *Ibid.*, 285.
9. *Ibid.*, 274.
10. *Ibid.*, 262–3.
11. *Ibid.*, 274–5.
12. Dee Brown, *Bury My Heart at Wounded Knee* (New York: Pocket Books, 1981), 300.
13. Brown, *Bury My Heart at Wounded Knee*, 262.
14. Clifford Geertz, "The impact of the concept of culture on the concept of man", *The Interpretation of Cultures*, 46, 49.
15. *Ibid.*, 49.
16. See Robert D. Putnam, *Bowling Alone: The Collapse and Revival of American Community* (New York: Simon & Schuster, 2000).
17. Emily Dickinson, poem 303, *The Complete Poems of Emily Dickinson*, ed. T. Johnson (Boston, MA: Little, Brown, 1960), 143.
18. Locke, *The Second Treatise*, 276.
19. Adam Smith, *The Theory of Moral Sentiments*, ed. K. Haakonssen (Cambridge: Cambridge University Press, 2002), 11.
20. Jeremy Bentham, "Nonsense upon stilts", in *Selected Writings* (New Haven, CT: Yale University Press, 2011), 328.
21. Jeremy Bentham, *An Introduction to the Principles of Morals and Legislation* (Mineola, NY: Dover Publications, 2007), 2.
22. *Ibid.*, 4.
23. *Ibid.*, 29.
24. *Ibid.*, 31.
25. J. J. C. Smart and Bernard Williams, *Utilitarianism: For and Against* (Cambridge: Cambridge University Press, 1973).
26. Thomas Cathcart, *The Trolley Problem, or Would You Throw the Fat Guy Off the Bridge?* (New York: Workman Publishing, 2013).
27. J. S. Mill, *On Liberty and Other Writings*, ed. S. Collini (Cambridge: Cambridge University Press, 1989), 57, 56.
28. *Ibid.*, 58.
29. *Ibid.*, 59.

30. *Ibid.*, 13.
31. See Bevir & Blakely, *Interpretive Social Science*, 36–40.

2 OTHER FOUNDINGS: CIVIC REPUBLICANISM AND WHITE SUPREMACY

1. James Q. Whitman, *Hitler's American Model: The United States and the Making of Nazi Race Law* (Princeton, NJ: Princeton University Press, 2017).
2. Alexis de Tocqueville, *Democracy in America*, trans. G. Lawrence, ed. J. P. Mayer (New York: HarperCollins, 2000), 279.
3. Jean-Jacques Rousseau, *The Social Contract and Other Later Political Writings*, trans. V. Gourevitch (Cambridge: Cambridge University Press, 1997), 113.
4. Aristotle, *The Politics*, trans. C. Lord (Chicago, IL: University of Chicago Press, 1985), 1253a.
5. Tocqueville, *Democracy in America*, 508.
6. *Ibid.*, 692.
7. Putnam, *Bowling Alone*.
8. Plato, "Apology" in *Five Dialogues*, second edition, trans. G. M. A. Grube (Indianapolis, IN: Hackett, 2002).
9. Harvey C. Mansfield, *Tocqueville: A Very Short Introduction* (Oxford: Oxford University Press, 2010), 3.
10. *Ibid.*; Robert Bellah *et al.*, "Taming the savage market", *The Christian Century* 108:26 (Sep 1991), 844–9.
11. Malcolm X, *The Autobiography of Malcolm X: As Told to Alex Haley* (New York: Ballantine, 1964), 205.
12. Tocqueville, *Democracy in America*, 261.
13. Thomas Jefferson, "Thomas Jefferson's thoughts on the negro: part I", *The Journal of Negro History* 3:1 (1918), 68.
14. *Ibid.*, 65.
15. *Ibid.*
16. *Ibid.*, 66.
17. *Ibid.*, 65.
18. Richard J. Herrnstein and Charles Murray, *The Bell Curve: Intelligence and Class Structure in American Life* (New York: Simon & Schuster, 1994); James Q. Wilson and Richard Herrnstein, *Crime and Human Nature* (New York: Simon & Schuster, 1985).
19. See Blakely, *We Built Reality*, 100–101.
20. James Baldwin and Nikki Giovanni, *A Dialogue* (Philadelphia, PA: Lippincott, 1973), 70–71.
21. John Calhoun, "Speech on the reception of abolition petitions [February 6, 1837]", in *Union and Liberty: The Political Philosophy of John C. Calhoun*, ed. R. Lence (Indianapolis, IN: Liberty Fund, 1992), 474.
22. See Calhoun, "Speech on the reception of abolition petitions", 470–71.
23. John Calhoun, *A Disquisition on Government*, in *Union and Liberty*, 3.

24. *Ibid.*, 21.
25. *Ibid.*, 22.
26. Michelle Alexander, *The New Jim Crow* (New York: The New Press, 2010).

3 DUELING LIBERALISMS: PROGRESSIVES VERSUS RIGHT LIBERTARIANS

1. T. H. Green, "Lecture on liberal legislation and freedom of contract", *Works of Thomas Hill Green*, vol. 3, ed. R. L. Nettleship (Cambridge: Cambridge University Press, 2011), 365–86.
2. *Ibid.*, 374.
3. Franklin Delano Roosevelt, "State of the Union message to Congress, January 11, 1944", Franklin D. Roosevelt Presidential Library and Museum; https://www.fdrlibrary.org/address-text.
4. John Steinbeck, *The Grapes of Wrath and Other Writings* (New York: Library of America, 1996); John Steinbeck, "Starvation under the orange trees", in *America and Americans and Selected Nonfiction*, eds S. Shillinglaw and J. Benson (New York: Viking, 2002), 85.
5. John Dewey, "The future of liberalism", in *The Later Works of John Dewey, Volume 11: 1935–1937*, ed. J. A. Boydston (Carbondale, IL: Southern Illinois University Press), 292.
6. Milton Friedman, "Capitalism and freedom", *New Individualist Review* 1:1 (1961), 3.
7. *Ibid.*
8. Milton Friedman, "Neo-liberalism and its prospects", in *The Indispensable Milton Friedman*, ed. L. Ebenstein (Washington, DC: Regnery, 2012), 7.
9. *Ibid.*
10. Smith, *The Theory of Moral Sentiments*, 120.
11. Gordon Wood, *The Radicalism of the American Revolution* (New York: Vintage, 1991), 106–107.
12. F. A. Hayek, "Freedom and economic system", in *Socialism and War: Essays, Documents, Reviews, Volume 10, The Collected Works of F. A. Hayek*, B. Caldwell ed. (Chicago, IL: University of Chicago Press, 1997), 183, 182, 185.
13. See Jason Blakely, "How economics becomes ideology: the uses and abuses of rational choice theory", in *Agency and Causal Explanation in Economics*, eds P. Róna and L. Zsolnai (Cham: Springer, 2020), 37–52.
14. James M. Buchanan, "The Samaritan's dilemma", in *Altruism, Morality, and Economic Theory*, ed. E. Phelps (New York: Russell Sage Foundation, 1975), 75.
15. James M. Buchanan, "Why does government grow?" in *Budgets and Bureaucrats: The Source of Government Growth*, ed. T. Borherding (Durham, NC: Duke University Press, 1977), 11, 13, 3.
16. *Ibid.*, 9.
17. *Ibid.*, 17.

18. For the neoliberal transformation of the state, see Mark Bevir, *Democratic Governance* (Princeton, NJ: Princeton University Press, 2010), 15–92.
19. James Buchanan and Gordon Tullock, *The Collected Works of James M. Buchanan, Volume 3: The Calculus of Consent* (Indianapolis, IN: Liberty Fund, 1999), 12, 14.
20. "Margaret Thatcher: a life in quotes", *The Guardian*, 8 April 2013; https://www.theguardian.com/politics/2013/apr/08/margaret-thatcher-quotes.
21. Steven Roberts, "Ronald Reagan is giving 'em heck", *New York Times*, 25 October 1970, 22.
22. Ronald Reagan, "Radio address to the nation on welfare reform, August 1, 1987" Online by G. Peters and J. T. Woolley, The American Presidency Project; https://www.presidency.ucsb.edu/node/252717.
23. For example, see Amos Tversky and Daniel Kahneman, "Advances in prospect theory: cumulative representation of uncertainty", *Journal of Risk and Uncertainty* 5(1992), 298.
24. Milton Friedman, *Capitalism and Freedom*, fortieth anniversary edn (Chicago, IL: University of Chicago Press, 2002), 9.
25. Ayn Rand, *Atlas Shrugged* (New York: Plume, 1999), 1139.
26. Ayn Rand, *The Virtue of Selfishness: A New Concept of Egoism* (New York: Signet, 1964).
27. Robert Nozick, *Anarchy, State and Utopia* (New York: Basic Books, 1974), 172.

4 IN THE NAME OF THE PAST: CONSERVATISM'S MULTIPLE TRADITIONS

1. William F. Buckley, Jr. "National Review: Credenda and Statement of Principles", in *Conservatism in America since 1930: A Reader*, ed. G. Schneider (New York: New York University Press, 2003), 201.
2. Edmund Burke, *Reflections on the Revolution in France*, in *Select Works of Edmund Burke, Volume 2*, ed. F. Canavan (Indianapolis, IN: Liberty Fund, 1999), 108.
3. *Ibid.*, 172.
4. *Ibid.*, 169.
5. *Ibid.*, 171.
6. See Taylor, *A Secular Age*.
7. Burke, *Reflections on the Revolution in France*, 193.
8. *Ibid.*, 192.
9. Douglas Murray, *Neoconservatism: Why We Need It* (San Francisco, CA: Encounter, 2006), 34.
10. Roger Scruton, *How to be a Conservative* (London: Bloomsbury, 2014), ix, viii.
11. Burke, *Reflections on the Revolution in France*, 191.
12. *Ibid.*, 149, 151.

13. Michael Oakeshott, *Rationalism in Politics and Other Essays* (Indianapolis, IN: Liberty Fund, 1991).
14. T. S. Eliot, "The Wasteland", in *The Complete Poems and Plays: 1909–1950* (New York: Harcourt, Brace, 1952), 38.
15. Twelve Southerners, *I'll Take My Stand: The South and the Agrarian Tradition* (Baton Rouge, LA: Louisiana State University Press, 1962), xxxvii, xxxix.
16. F. A. Hayek, "Why I am not a conservative", in *The Constitution of Liberty* in *The Collected Works of F. A. Hayek*, Volume 17, ed. R. Hamowy (Chicago, IL: University of Chicago Press, 2011), 520.
17. Burke, *Reflections on the Revolution in France*, 169.
18. Laurence Jurdem, "Reagan and his favorite magazine", *National Review*, 5 December 2015; https://www.nationalreview.com/2015/12/paving-way-reagan/.
19. Buckley, "National Review: Credenda and Statement of Principles", 204.
20. *Ibid.*, 203–204.
21. Michael Flamm, *Law and Order: Street Crime, Civil Unrest, and the Crisis of Liberalism in the 1960s* (New York: Columbia University Press, 2005), 64.
22. William F. Buckley, "Why the South must prevail", *National Review* 24 (1957), 148–9.
23. Irving Kristol, "Capitalism, socialism, and nihilism", *The Public Interest* 31 (1973), 12.
24. *Ibid.*, 11.
25. Leo Strauss, "The three waves of modernity", in *An Introduction to Political Philosophy: Ten Essays by Leo Strauss*, ed. H. Gildin (Detroit, MI: Wayne State University Press, 1989), 81–98.
26. Jason Blakely, "Nihilism as rightwing political rhetoric", *Theory & Event* 22:1 (2019), 92–114.
27. For the background to this movement, see Irving Kristol, "A conservative welfare state", in *The Essential Neoconservative Reader*, ed. M. Gerson (Reading, MA: Addison-Wesley, 1996), 285.

5 THERE IS NO "FASCIST MINIMUM": FASCIST BUNDLES AND HYBRIDIZATIONS

1. Tony Judt (with Timothy Snyder), *Thinking the Twentieth Century* (New York: Penguin, 2012), 159.
2. Carl Schmitt, *The Concept of the Political*, trans. G. Schwab (Chicago, IL: University of Chicago Press, 2007), 26.
3. Umberto Eco, "Ur-Fascism", in *Five Moral Pieces*, trans. A. McEwen (New York: Harcourt, 2001), 77, 80.
4. Cf. Roger Griffin, "General introduction", in *Fascism*, ed. R. Griffin (Oxford: Oxford University Press, 1995), 2–4; Robert Paxton, *The Anatomy of Fascism* (New York: Vintage, 2005), 9–15.

5. Ludwig Wittgenstein, *Philosophical Investigations*, third edn, trans. G. E. M. Anscombe (Oxford: Blackwell, 2001) §67.
6. See Roger Griffin, *Fascism* (Cambridge: Polity, 2018).
7. See Jeffrey Herf, *Reactionary Modernism: Technology, Culture, and Politics in Weimar and the Third Reich* (Cambridge: Cambridge University Press, 1984); Fritz Stern, *The Politics of Cultural Despair: A Study in the Rise of the Germanic Ideology* (Berkeley, CA: University of California Press, 1989).
8. Cf. A. James Gregor, *Giovanni Gentile: Philosopher of Fascism* (New Brunswick, NJ: Transaction, 2001), xii–xiii, 100.
9. Martin Heidegger, *The Question Concerning Technology and Other Essays*, trans. W. Lovitt (New York: Garland, 1977), 28.
10. Martin Heidegger, *Introduction to Metaphysics*, trans. G. Fried and R. Polt (New Haven, CT: Yale University Press, 2000), 213.
11. See Hannah Arendt, *The Origins of Totalitarianism* (New York: Harcourt, 1976).
12. See Jacob Golomb and Robert S. Wistrich, eds, *Nietzsche, Godfather of Fascism?* (Princeton, NJ: Princeton University Press, 2002).
13. Benito Mussolini and Giovanni Gentile, "Foundations and doctrine of fascism", in *A Primer of Italian Fascism*, ed. J. Schnapp (Lincoln, NE: University of Nebraska Press, 2000), 54.
14. Eline Schaart, "Matteo Salvini quotes controversial fascist-era poet", Politico, 5 March 2019; https://www.politico.eu/article/matteo-salvini-ezra-pound-quotes-controversial-fascist-era-poet/.
15. Carl Schmitt, "The legal basis of the total state", in *Fascism*, ed. R. Griffin, 138.
16. Oswald Mosley, "Ten points of fascist policy", in *Political Ideologies*, eds, M. Festenstein and M. Kenny (Oxford: Oxford University Press, 2005), 397.
17. Schmitt, *The Concept of the Political*, 27.
18. *Ibid.*, 53.
19. Mussolini & Gentile, "Foundations and doctrine of fascism", 53.
20. Carl Schmitt, "Dialogue on new space", in *Dialogues on Power and Space*, eds A. Kalyvas and F. Finchelstein, trans. S. Zeitlin (Cambridge: Polity, 2015), 54; Enzo Traverso, *Fire and Blood: The European Civil War 1914–1945*, trans. D. Fernbach (London: Verso, 2016), 41, 61; Stanley G. Payne, *A History of Fascism, 1914–1945* (Madison, WI: University of Wisconsin Press, 1995), 157–8.
21. Mosley, "Ten points of fascist policy", 396–7.
22. Paxton, *The Anatomy of Fascism*, 10.
23. Carl Schmitt, *Political Theology: Four Chapters on the Concept of Sovereignty* (Cambridge, MA: MIT Press, 1985), 36.
24. Mosley, "Ten points of fascist policy", 397.
25. Schmitt, *Political Theology*, 38, 12.
26. *Ibid.*, 5.
27. Carl Schmitt, "Dialogue on power and access to the holder of power", in *Dialogues on Power and Space*, 47, 41.

28. Arendt, *The Origins of Totalitarianism*, 375.
29. See Aristotle, *Politics*, Book 1.
30. Paxton, *The Anatomy of Fascism*, 202.
31. *Ibid.*, 201.
32. See Jason Blakely, "Teaching Trump to college students", *The Atlantic*, 31 August 2016; https://www.theatlantic.com/education/archive/2016/08/teaching-trump-to-college-students/498158/.
33. Robert P. Ericksen, *Theologians Under Hitler* (New Haven, CT: Yale University Press, 1985).
34. Chris Hedges, *American Fascists: The Christian Right and the War on America* (New York: Simon & Schuster, 2006), 10–13.
35. Rod Dreher, "Trump the *katechon*", *The American Conservative*, 13 February 2019; https://www.theamericanconservative.com/trump-the-katechon/.
36. Traverso, *Fire and Blood*, 262. Schmitt's influence is also evident in the Catholic "integralist" circles formed around the Harvard law professor, Adrian Vermeule. For this ideology as fascist adjacent, see Jason Blakely, "Cass Sunstein and Adrian Vermeule's technocratic despotism", *Chronicle of Higher Education*, 1 February 2021; www.chronicle.com/article/cass-sunstein-and-adrian-vermeules-technocratic-despotism and "Not Catholic enough: the integralism of Adrian Vermeule", *Commonweal* 147:9 (2020), 34–47.
37. Michael Anton (Publius Decius Mus), "The Flight 93 Election", *Claremont Review of Books*, 5 September 2016; https://claremontreviewofbooks.com/digital/the-flight-93-election/.
38. Jason Wilson, "'Red Caesarism' is rightwing code", *The Guardian*, 1 October 2023; https://www.theguardian.com/world/2023/oct/01/red-caesar-authoritarianism-republicans-extreme-right.
39. Cf. Dylan Matthews, "Is Trump a fascist? 8 experts weigh in", Vox, 23 October 2020; https://www.vox.com/policy-and-politics/21521958/what-is-fascism-signs-donald-trump.

6 IS SOCIALISM STILL TABOO? FROM MARXISM TO BERNIE SANDERS

1. Michael Harrington, *Socialism: Past and Future* (New York: Arcade, 2011), 3.
2. Karl Marx and Friedrich Engels, *The German Ideology* (New York: Prometheus, 1998), 264.
3. Karl Marx, "Theses on Feuerbach", in *The Marx-Engels Reader*, second edn, R. Tucker, ed. (New York: Norton, 1978), 145.
4. Karl Marx and Friedrich Engels, "Manifesto of the Communist Party", in *The Marx-Engels Reader*, 479.
5. *Ibid.*, 486.
6. *Ibid.*, 479.
7. *Ibid.*, 485.

8. See Mark Fisher, *Capitalist Realism* (Alresford: Zero Books, 2009), 19, 25, 35–7.
9. Marx & Engels, "Manifesto of the Communist Party", 476.
10. *Ibid.*, 483.
11. In what follows I draw on Charles Taylor, "Marxist philosophy: dialogue with Charles Taylor", in *Men of Ideas: Some Creators of Contemporary Philosophy*, ed. B. Magee (London: BBC, 1978) 42–58.
12. Jack London, "How I became a socialist", in *The Radical Jack London*, ed. J. Raskin (Berkeley, CA: University of California Press, 2008), 124, 126.
13. Joseph Stalin, *Dialectical and Historical Materialism* (New York: International Publishers, 1940), 15.
14. Eugene V. Debs, "The eight hour work day", *International Socialist Review* 12:2 (1911), 100–101.
15. Robert Bellah, "The American taboo on socialism", in *The Broken Covenant*, second edn (Chicago, IL: University of Chicago Press, 1992), 114.
16. Fisher, *Capitalist Realism*, 2.
17. Cf. Mark Bevir, *The Making of British Socialism* (Princeton, NJ: Princeton University Press, 2011).
18. Eduard Bernstein, *Evolutionary Socialism: A Criticism and Affirmation*, trans. E. Harvey (New York: Schocken Books, 1967), 145.
19. Irving Howe, "Socialism and liberalism: articles of conciliation?" *Dissent* 24 (Winter 1977), 22–35.
20. Harrington, *Socialism*, 248–9.
21. *Ibid.*, 265.
22. *Ibid.*, 273.
23. George Orwell, *The Road to Wigan Pier* (New York: Harcourt, Brace, 1958), 203.
24. Marx & Engels, "Manifesto of the Communist Party", 498.
25. Erik Olin Wright, *Envisioning Real Utopias* (London: Verso, 2010), 121.
26. *Ibid.*, 122.
27. Marx & Engels, "Manifesto of the Communist Party", 490.
28. *Ibid.*, 486.
29. Wright, *Envisioning Real Utopias*, 155–8.
30. Some prominent millennial socialists have seemed to echo this approach: Bhaskar Sunkara, *The Socialist Manifesto* (New York: Basic Books, 2019).
31. Fredric Jameson, *An American Utopia: Dual Power and the Universal Army*, ed. S. Žižek (London: Verso, 2016), 19.
32. *Ibid.*, 62, 35.

7 HIDING IN PLAIN SIGHT: NATIONALISM AND MULTICULTURALISM

1. Bevir, *The Making of British Socialism*, 90–92.
2. In the United States both progressives and conservatives have at times claimed nationalism as their own: Richard Rorty, "American

national pride: Whitman and Dewey", in *Achieving Our Country: Leftist Thought in Twentieth-Century America* (Cambridge, MA: Harvard University Press, 1998), 1–38; Yuval Levin, "Burke and the nation", *Law & Liberty*, 19 July 2019; https://lawliberty.org/burke-and-the-nation/.

3. Chris Hedges, *War Is A Force That Gives Us Meaning* (New York: Public Affairs, 2002), 32.
4. Heinrich von Treitschke, *Politics*, vol. 1, trans. B. Dugdale and T. de Bille (New York: Macmillan, 1916), 271.
5. *Ibid.*, 280.
6. *Ibid.*, 270.
7. *Ibid.*, 272, 273.
8. Max Weber, "Politics as a vocation", in *The Vocation Lectures*, trans. R. Livingstone; eds D. Owen and T. Strong (Indianapolis, IN: Hackett, 2004), 33.
9. Treitschke, *Politics*, 291, 293.
10. *Ibid.*, 280.
11. Benedict Anderson, *Imagined Communities: Reflections on the Origin and Spread of Nationalism* (London: Verso, 2006).
12. Charles Taylor, "Nationalism and modernity", in *Dilemmas and Connections* (Cambridge, MA: Harvard University Press, 2011), 91.
13. Eugen Weber, *Peasants into Frenchmen: The Modernization of Rural France, 1870–1914* (Stanford, CA: Stanford University Press, 1976).
14. What follows draws on a longer analysis in Taylor, "Nationalism and modernity", 81–104.
15. Gordon S. Wood, *The Radicalism of the American Revolution* (New York: Vintage, 1991), 222.
16. Jean-Jacques Rousseau, *Considerations on the Government of Poland* in *The Social Contract and Other Later Political Writings*, ed. V. Gourevitch (Cambridge: Cambridge University Press, 1997), 193, 187.
17. *Ibid.*, 183.
18. *Ibid.*, 187, 188.
19. Ralph Waldo Emerson, *The Journals and Miscellaneous Notebooks of Ralph Waldo Emerson*, vol. IX: 1843–47, ed. R. Orth and A. Ferguson (Cambridge, MA: Harvard University Press, 1971), 299–300.
20. See Sarah Wayland, "Immigration, multiculturalism and national identity in Canada", *International Journal on Minority and Group Rights* 5:1 (1997), 33–58.
21. Will Kymlicka, *Multicultural Citizenship: A Liberal Theory of Minority Rights* (Oxford: Oxford University Press, 1995), 7–9.
22. See also Kymlicka's typology of "group-differentiated rights": *Multicultural Citizenship*, 6–7, 26–33.
23. Kymlicka, *Multicultural Citizenship*, 7.
24. Charles Taylor, "The politics of recognition", in *Multiculturalism: Examining the Politics of Recognition*, ed. A. Gutmann (Princeton, NJ: Princeton University Press, 1994), 25–6.

25. Taylor, *A Secular Age*, 303.
26. Taylor, "The politics of recognition", 52.
27. *Ibid.*, 52–3.
28. Ian Schwartz, "Cornel West: America is a failed social experiment, neoliberal wing of Democratic Party must be fought", *Real Clear Politics*, 29 May 2020; https://www.realclearpolitics.com/video/2020/05/29/cornel_west_america_is_a_failed_social_experiment_neoliberal_wing_of_democratic_party_must_be_fought.html.
29. Cf. Twelve Southerners, *I'll Take My Stand*.
30. For how the latter might be formulated, see Jason Blakely, "Radicalizing and de-radicalizing Charles Taylor", *International Journal of Philosophical Studies* 29:5 (2021), 693–4. Richard Rorty, by contrast, criticized multiculturalism for replacing a politics of material equality with the symbolic "politics of difference"; Rorty, *Achieving Our Country*, 76–7.
31. Susan Moller Okin, *Is Multiculturalism Bad for Women?* eds J. Cohen, M. Howard and M. Nussbaum (Princeton, NJ: Princeton University Press, 1999), 10.
32. Okin, *Is Multiculturalism Bad for Women?*, 14.
33. Charles Taylor, "Conditions of an unforced consensus on human rights", in *Dilemmas and Connections*, 123.
34. Mark Lilla, *The Once and Future Liberal: After Identity Politics* (London: Hurst, 2018), 132–3.

8 THERE ARE MANY FEMINISMS: THE ADVENT OF SEXUAL POLITICS

1. Mary Wollstonecraft, *A Vindication of the Rights of Woman*, ed. E. Botting (New Haven, CT: Yale University Press, 2014), 23.
2. Elizabeth Cady Stanton, "Declaration of sentiments" in *The Selected Papers of Elizabeth Cady Stanton and Susan B. Anthony* (New Brunswick, NJ: Rutgers University Press, 1997), 78.
3. Wollstonecraft, *Vindication of the Rights of Woman*, 45.
4. *Ibid.*, 60–61.
5. "First Annual Catalogue of the Officers and Students of Vassar Female College" (New York: John A. Gray & Green, 1866), 16.
6. Wollstonecraft, *Vindication of the Rights of Woman*, 24.
7. For example, see Robert Bellah *et al.*'s description of the evangelical Christian conception of marriage in the 1980s as among the most patriarchal in the United States but nonetheless not wholly "immune to pressures for the equality of women". Robert Bellah *et al.*, *Habits of the Heart: Individualism and Commitment in American Life* (Berkeley, CA: University of California Press, 1985), 97, 85–112.
8. For a recent critical treatment of this trope, see Sara Ahmed, "Feminist killjoys (and other willful subjects)", *S&F Online* 8.3 (Summer 2010), Barnard Center for Research on Women; https://sfonline.barnard.edu/polyphonic/ahmed_01.htm.

9. Simone de Beauvoir, *The Second Sex*, trans. C. Borde (New York: Vintage, 2011), 283.
10. Betty Friedan, *The Feminine Mystique* (New York: Norton, 1997), 433.
11. Sylvia Plath, "Daddy", in *Collected Poems*, ed. T. Hughes (New York: Harper Perennial, 1992), 223.
12. Kate Millett, *Sexual Politics* (New York: Columbia University Press, 2016), 25.
13. *Ibid.*, 25.
14. *Ibid.*
15. Catharine A. MacKinnon, *Toward a Feminist Theory of the State* (Cambridge, MA: Harvard University Press, 1989), 124.
16. Millett, *Sexual Politics*, 44.
17. *Ibid.*, 26.
18. *Ibid.*, 31.
19. *Ibid.*, 24–5.
20. Judith Butler, *Gender Trouble: Feminism and the Subversion of Identity* (London: Routledge, 1990), 1, 4.
21. *Ibid.*, 3; Judith Butler, "Performative acts and gender constitution: an essay in phenomenology and feminist theory", *Theatre Journal* 40:4 (1998), 529.
22. Butler, *Gender Trouble*, 7.
23. For a roundup of some of these philosophical arguments, see Georgia Warnke, "The woman subject", *Aeon*, 10 April 2019; https://aeon.co/essays/do-analytic-and-continental-philosophy-agree-what-woman-is.
24. Georgia Warnke, *Debating Sex and Gender* (Oxford: Oxford University Press, 2011), vii.
25. Camille Paglia, *Vamps & Tramps* (New York: Random House, 1994), 110.
26. See, for example, Camille Paglia, "Madonna – finally, a real feminist", *New York Times*, 14 December 1990.
27. bell hooks, *Feminism is for Everybody: Passionate Politics* (New York: Routledge, 2015), 55–6.
28. Butler, "Performative acts and gender constitution", 519.
29. Judith Butler, *Bodies That Matter: On the Discursive Limits of Sex* (New York: Routledge, 2011), ix.
30. *Ibid.*, 163.
31. Butler, *Gender Trouble*, 137.
32. Butler, "Performative acts and gender constitution", 524.
33. See, for example, Sally Haslanger, *Resisting Reality: Social Construction and Social Critique* (Oxford: Oxford University Press, 2012); Nancy Fraser, "Feminism, capitalism, and the cunning of history: an introduction", FMSH-WP-2012-17, August 2012.
34. Wendy Brown, "Women dissolved or defended? The naming debate in reproductive freedom", Pembroke Center, Brown University, YouTube, 18 March 2015; https://youtu.be/D2Eop1_T02s.
35. See Michaele Ferguson, "Neoliberal feminism as political ideology",

Journal of Political Ideologies 22:3 (2017), 221–35; Linda Hirshman, "Homeward bound", *The American Prospect*, 22 November 2005; Linda Hirshman, *Get to Work: A Manifesto for Women of the World* (New York: Viking, 2006), 10.

36. Jon Pareles, "Finding her future looking to the past", *New York Times*, 12 June 2014; https://www.nytimes.com/2014/06/15/arts/music/lana-del-rey-still-stirs-things-up-with-ultraviolence.html?_r=0.
37. Geertz, "The impact of the concept of culture on the concept of man", 46, 49.

9 THE MEANING OF THE EARTH: THE CHALLENGES OF ECOLOGICAL POLITICS

1. Locke, *The Second Treatise of Government*, 282.
2. Karl Marx, *Capital: A Critique of Political Economy*, vol. 3, ed. F. Engels, trans. E. Untermann (Chicago, IL: Charles Kerr & Co., 1909), 954.
3. Marx & Engels, "Manifesto of the Communist Party", 474, 476.
4. See Charles Taylor, *The Language Animal: The Full Shape of the Human Linguistic Capacity* (Cambridge, MA: Harvard University Press, 2016).
5. Walt Whitman, "When I heard the learn'd astronomer", in *Leaves of Grass* (Philadelphia, PA: David McKay, 1891–92), 214.
6. John Muir, "Man's place in the universe", in *A Thousand-Mile Walk to the Gulf* (1916); http://www.yosemite.ca.us/john_muir_writings/mans_place_in_the_universe.html.
7. Henry David Thoreau, *Walden; or, Life in the Woods*, in the *The Portable Thoreau*, ed. C. Bode (New York: Penguin, 1982), 343.
8. *Ibid.*, 344.
9. *Ibid.*, 345.
10. *Ibid.*, 263.
11. See Martin Heidegger, *The Question Concerning Technology*, trans. W. Lovitt (New York: Garland, 1977).
12. Hartmut Rosa, *The Uncontrollability of the World*, trans. J. C. Wagner (Cambridge: Polity, 2020), 20.
13. Arnae Næss, "The deep ecological movement: some philosophical aspects", *Philosophical Inquiry* 8:1/2 (1986), 10–31.
14. William Wordsworth, *The Major Works*, ed. S. Gill (Oxford: Oxford University Press, 1984), 303.
15. Joni Mitchell, *The Complete Poems and Lyrics* (New York: Crown, 1997), 56.
16. Wendell Berry, "Preserving wildness", in *American Earth: Environmental Writing Since Thoreau*, ed. B. McKibben (Boone, IA: Library of America, 2008), 523.
17. Rachel Carson, *Silent Spring*, fortieth anniversary edn (New York: Houghton Mifflin, 2002).
18. Craig Calhoun and Benjamin Fong, eds, *The Green New Deal and the Frontier of Work* (New York: Columbia University Press, 2022) 1, 8.
19. Fisher, *Capitalist Realism*, 18.

20. Murray Bookchin, "An ecological society", in *Murray Bookchin Reader* (Montreal, ON: Black Rose Books, 1999), 15.
21. *Ibid.*, 23.
22. See Janet Biehl and Peter Staudenmaier, *Ecofascism Revisited: Lessons from the German Experience*, second edn (Porsgrunn, Norway: New Compass Press, 2011).

CONCLUSION: THE AGE OF IDEOLOGIES

1. Plato, *Phaedo*, trans. H. Tredennick, in *Plato: Collected Dialogues*, eds E. Hamilton and H. Cairns (Princeton, NJ: Princeton University Press, 1989), 68.
2. Ricoeur, "Can there be a scientific concept of ideology?", 57–8.
3. Due to this incoherence, some political scientists argue that the American "public" is mostly "innocent of ideology". But this mistakenly equates eccentric, somewhat incoherent hybrids of ideology, with having no ideology at all; see Donald R. Kinder and Nathan P. Kalmoe, *Neither Liberal Nor Conservative: Ideological Innocence in the American Public* (Chicago, IL: University of Chicago Press, 2017), 47.
4. For more on an interpretive approach to understanding social reality, see Bevir & Blakely, *Interpretive Social Science*.
5. For the ways in which an interpretive social science is critical, see Bevir & Blakely, *Interpretive Social Science*, 30–31, 54–63, 143–4, 162–79.
6. Blakely, *We Built Reality*.
7. This means that claims like those made by Francis Fukuyama – that liberalism is "free" of "fundamental internal contradictions" – are misleading at best. Francis Fukuyama, "By way of an introduction", *The End of History and the Last Man* (New York: Free Press, 1992), xi.
8. Charles Taylor, *Sources of the Self* (Cambridge: Cambridge University Press, 1989); Charles Taylor, *The Ethics of Authenticity* (Cambridge, MA: Harvard University Press, 1991).
9. Ricoeur, "Can there be a scientific concept of ideology?", 59.
10. Malcolm X, "Message to the grassroots, November 10, 1963," in *Malcolm X Speaks: Selected Speeches and Statements*, ed. George Breitman (New York: Grove Press, 1990), 10–11.

Index